I0881703

THE SPIRIT OF GOD

THE SPIRIT OF GOD

By the Rev.

G. CAMPBELL MORGAN

Author of *God's Methods with Man, The Hidden Years at Nazareth, Discipleship Life Problems*

Wipf and Stock Publishers
EUGENE, OREGON

Wipf and Stock Publishers
199 West 8th Avenue, Suite 3
Eugene, Oregon 97401

The Spirit of God
By Morgan, G. C.
Copyright©1900 by Morgan, G. C.
ISBN: 1-59244-342-7
Publication date 9/12/2003
Previously published by Fleming H. Revell Company, 1900

To

THE FRAGRANT MEMORY OF

GEORGE H. C. MACGREGOR, M.A.

WHO IS NOW AMONG THOSE WHO KNOW

IN THE LIGHT OF THE

SEVEN SPIRITS BEFORE THE THRONE

AND

IN COMRADESHIP AND COMMUNION WITH WHOM

THE IDEA OF SUCH A TREATISE WAS SUGGESTED

I DEDICATE THESE PAGES

In this age of faith in the natural, and disinclination to the supernatural, we want especially to meet the whole world with this credo: "I believe in the Holy Ghost."

WILLIAM ARTHUR.

CONTENTS

INTRODUCTORY

BOOK I

THE SPIRIT OF GOD

BOOK II

IDEAL CREATION

BOOK III

THE SPIRIT PRIOR TO PENTECOST

BOOK IV

THE TEACHING OF CHRIST CONCERNING THE SPIRIT

BOOK V

THE PENTECOSTAL AGE

BOOK VI

THE SPIRIT IN THE INDIVIDUAL

BOOK VII

THE PRACTICAL APPLICATION

NOTE.—The Revised Version is used, and the term *Holy Spirit* in preference to *Holy Ghost*.

INTRODUCTORY

SIGNS OF THE TIMES

DURING recent years two movements have been noticeable in the thought of men outside the Christian Church. First, there has been the development of materialism. The teachings of Darwin, Huxley, Tyndall, and Spencer have tended to the denial of the spiritual in man. Thousands of people who have never read their books have been influenced by their outlook upon life. Moreover, a great many of their first positions have been accepted and taught, and are held until this moment, without any due allowance being made for subsequent statements, which have proved that their teaching consisted in the suggestion of hypotheses, rather than the declaration of ascertained facts. According to such teachers all the phenomena of human life are to be accounted for wholly within the range of matter. It is admitted by them that matter is in itself indestructible; but it is affirmed that the rearrangement of it that takes place at death destroys the identity of human beings. In a more cultured and refined form, and with gleams of hope in the form of doubts, men have been gradually drifting towards materialism; and the effect of this has been seen in the average human life apart from the influence and teaching of Christianity. *Earthly, sensual, devilish,*[1] are words which fitly describe the vast mass of life apart from God. Some of the old forms of fleshly life have indeed ceased, and there is in the minds of men a new respect for personal character, as a result of the presence of Christianity in the world. A correct view of the condition of the masses of the race would reveal the fact that for the most part life is being lived in the realm of the fleshly, the material, the perishing. Thousands of men, while professing to hold the orthodox creed, are yet living in a practical atheism, and a consequent denial of their own spiritual nature.

The second movement outside the Church has taken the form of a revolt against materialism, and has found its expression in attempts to discover the spiritual—to unfold its laws, and to declare its activities. Spiritualism and theosophy are witnesses to this movement. Mrs. Annie Besant is one of the most remarkable instances of it in individual life. There was a time when she—sickened, alas! by the inconsistencies with which she came into contact within what was called, and falsely called, Christianity—turned her back upon the faith of her early years. She found refuge in denial of

[1] Jas. ii. 15.

high and sacred things; and lived wholly, to all appearance, outside the realm of the spiritual. For her to have found her way back to the acknowledgment of the spiritual in any form is a gain. It is, however, a remarkable fact that one who might have been spoken of as the high-priestess of materialism, in a rebound from that position, has taken a leap into the realm of credulity. Belief in a Mahatma, somewhere amid Himalayan heights, who has never been seen, requires a stretch of credence far greater than a belief in the living Christ of God, Whose presence on the earth nineteen hundred years ago is an indisputable historical fact, and Whose abiding presence is witnessed by innumerable transformations of character during the centuries.

This change of front on the part of so gifted a woman is a startling illustration of the fact that, side by side with the materialistic movement that has characterized the past half-century, there has also been a marked revolt against that movement. Indeed, the revolt against materialism has carried a certain section of the community into the opposite extreme. They are declaring that matter is not, and only mind really exists. The tendency of the past was to deny spirit. That has been proved to be absolutely untenable, and now it is the fashion to deny matter. This is evidenced by the vagaries of Christian science falsely so called

This groping in the darkness without, has had its

counterpart within the churches. A wave of rationalism, originating largely in Germany, has been sweeping over the religious world. Its effect has been the swamping of spiritual ideas and the extinguishing of the fires of Christian zeal. There are churches utterly devoid of the true spiritual tokens of men and women converted to God, and transformed into the likeness of Jesus Christ. Such churches, being destitute of the compassion of the Christ for the needs of men, all too sadly prove that the materialistic element, has crept within their borders, in the form of rationalistic theology, the canker-worm of spiritual life.

But just as outside the Church there has been a spirit of revolt, so within, contemporary with this rationalistic movement, there has been manifested a marked and wonderful revival of interest in the ministry of the Holy Spirit. In 1856 William Arthur issued his *Tongue of Fire.* It was indeed a fiery message to the churches; but it was before its time. Not that it was out of place. Every great movement has its forerunner. Every great development of thought starts with some lonely watchman upon the mountain, who catches the first ray of coming day, and tells the dwellers in the valley of its approach. The book was, in that sense, a book before its time; yet men read it—our fathers tell us—on their knees. There followed a period of waiting, a time during which it appeared as though the book were dead. It was dead as the seed-corn dies, only to issue in a glorious harvest. During the last quarter of the century, men in all sections of the Christian Church have spoken and written upon this great theme of the ministry and work of the Holy Spirit. Dr. Scofield, of Northfield, says: *More books, booklets, and tracts upon that subject have issued from the press during the last twenty years than in all the time since the invention of printing.* The truth thus proclaimed has resulted in new life within the churches; and everywhere eager souls are enquiring after fuller, more definite, more systematic knowledge of this great ministry of the Spirit. The ministries that are forceful in the accomplishment of definite results in the interests of the kingdom of God today, are the ministries of men who are putting the whole burden of their work upon the Holy Spirit of God,—of men who, however different the subjects with which they deal, and however different their theological outlook may be in certain respects, are nevertheless perpetually realizing that the Holy Spirit is to be thought and spoken of as a Person rather than an influence. Wherever the Spirit of God is being enthroned in preaching and in all Christian work, and having His rightful place as the Administrator of the things of Jesus Christ, apostolic results are seen to follow.

Here, however, as always in the history of fallen man, the Divine movement has had its counterfeit.

The devil has two methods of procedure with regard to the living truth of God. First, he seeks to hide the vision. When that is no longer possible, when truth with its inherent brilliance and beauty is driving away the mists, then the devil's procedure is that of patronage and falsification. Taking it out of its true proportion, he turns it into deadly error.

The Reformation, for which we still thank God, was a return on the part of men, to whom God gave vision, to the great fundamental truth of justification by faith. The central gospel fact, *He that believeth on the Son hath eternal life,*[1] was rediscovered For long and weary years Satan had kept that truth out of sight; but when God raised up Martin Luther and others, the devil immediately adopted, adapted, and misapplied it. In the wake of the Reformation came the damnable heresy of antinomianism. Its teaching was, that if men are justified by faith, conduct is of no account; man sins perpetually, and nothing can alter the fact; but being justified by faith, the actual life and character are nothing. Thus a truth taken out of its proper setting, and stretched to undue proportions, became a heresy almost more fearful than that from which justification by faith was a deliverance.

Again, some years ago God raised up men to give renewed utterance to the truth of the premillennial coming of Jesus Christ. The effect produced was that of a purifying hope, and believers were recalled from worldliness and indifference, to the attitude of pilgrims girded for the King's business, and waiting for His

[1]John iii. 36.

appearing. Then immediately followed innumerable distortions of the truth by the powers of evil; and impertinent predictions of dates have almost brought it into general disrepute. Instead of the whole Church being purified, strengthened, and revived in prospect of events the time for which God Himself only knows, many are afraid to give any attention whatever to the subject, because it has been brought into disrepute by attempts to discover a date of which the Master said: *Of that day . . . knoweth no one, . . . not even . . . the Son.*[1]

Just as it was in these instances, so has it been in regard to the subject of the work of the Holy Spirit. The greatest peril which threatens the truth of the Spirit's personal ministry to-day, arises from the advocacy of the truth by those who are not careful to discover the mind of the Spirit. With the revival of interest there have been launched a number of wholly unauthorized systems, which have brought bondage where the Spirit would have brought liberty. Men have been misapplying phrases connected with this subject. The baptism of the Spirit, the anointing of the Spirit, the indwelling of the Spirit, the sealing of the Spirit, the filling of the Spirit—all these, based upon Scripture, have been taken out of their setting, and made the current phraseology of a new system of thought, which is a new form of legalism.

It is asserted, for instance, that a man who is con-

[1] Mark xiii. 32.

verted may be baptized of the Spirit, if—and then after the *if* comes the statement of certain conditions which constitute a legalism as disastrous as was that of the Judaizing teachers among the churches of Galatia. We are told that if a man will abandon this, that, and the other—and in many cases will cease to observe laws of life which are purely natural—he may be filled or baptized with the Spirit. All this is contrary to the teaching of the New Testament. The baptism of the Spirit is always used in the New Testament with reference to regeneration, and never with what is often spoken of to-day as *the second blessing.*

The filling of the Spirit through the fuller faith of the believer is often, but not necessarily a second blessing. All that is necessary for fuller realization of the Divine life becomes the birthright and property of believers directly they are born again of the Spirit of God. Nothing is more to be deprecated than the habit of formulating systems upon disjointed Scripture phrases apart from their connection with the context.

There is one sure and infallible guide to truth, and therefore one, and only one, corrective for error, and that is the Word of God. That, in this series of studies, is the court of appeal. May the Holy Spirit, without Whom there is no understanding of the Word, grant a clearer comprehension of His Person, of His work, and of human relation thereto! In approaching the subject the mind should be disabused of all foregone conclusions and prejudices, and a stand taken upon the old prophetic dictum: *To the law and to the testimony! if they speak not according to this word, surely there is no morning for them.*[1] There is no revelation of the activities of the Spirit of God, or of the spiritual world, save the revelation that comes through the Book.

[1] Isa. viii. 20.

BOOK I

THE SPIRIT OF GOD

Fountain of Love! Thyself true God!
Who through eternal days
From Father and from Son hast flow'd
In uncreated ways!

O Majesty unspeakable!
O Person all Divine!
How in the Threefold Majesty
Doth Thy Procession shine!

Proceeding, yet of equal age
With Those Whose love Thou art—
Proceeding, yet distinct, from Those
From Whom Thou seem'st to part.

An undivided Nature shared
With Father and with Son;
A Person by Thyself; with Them
Thy simple essence One.

Bond art Thou of the other Twain!
Omnipotent and free!
The consummating Love of God!
The Limit of the Three!

Thou art a Sea without a shore;
Awful, immense Thou art,—
A Sea which can contract itself
Within my narrow heart.

And yet Thou art a Haven, too,
Out on the shoreless sea,
A Harbour that can hold full well
Shipwreck'd Humanity.

Thou art an unborn Breath outbreathed
On angels and on men,
Subduing all things to Thyself,
We know not how or when.

O Light! O Love! O very God!
I dare not longer gaze
Upon Thy wondrous attributes
And their mysterious ways.

F. W. Faber.

II

THE PERSONALITY OF THE SPIRIT

BEFORE attempting to consider the work of the Holy Spirit through the history of the human race, it is necessary to understand, so far as it is possible, His personality and His relation to the Trinity. Only by a clear understanding of what the Scriptures teach concerning these matters, will it be at all possible to comprehend the mission and work of the Spirit.

Not that it is possible to perfectly understand the personality of the Spirit or His relation to the Trinity. These things are beyond the complete comprehension of minds that are finite. They must be accepted as declarations of a Divine revelation, the final explanation being impossible. It is possible and necessary to discover what the Scriptures of truth have declared about the Spirit in these two respects.

This chapter deals with the first point, the personality of the Spirit, under two divisions.

I. The Holy Spirit a Person.

II. The Holy Spirit a Divine Person.

The term *Person* immediately introduces an insurmountable difficulty—that, namely, of attempting to express the Infinite in finite terms.

It has been argued that personality and absolute existence are contradictions; that God cannot be, at one and the same time, a Person and Infinite. That argument is based upon the assumption that the term *Person* is capable of concise and final definition.

That is a false assumption. It supposes that perfect personality exists in a human being. This is not so. God alone has perfect personality. That of every other being is limited. In other words, God is not a magnified man, rather it may be said that man is a limited god. God is not in the image of man: man is in the image of God. Although, at first, it may appear as though this were a mere play upon words, yet a careful consideration of the statement will prove that no final and definite deductions concerning God can be made from a study of human life.

If man is the one, the final, the absolute unit, then the argument holds that God cannot be a Person and Infinite. If He alone be final and absolute, then personality in man is to be looked upon as being imperfect and limited. When a man declares God cannot be absolute and a Person, he does so because his only view of personality is the view which he has of himself or of his brother. It is possible to form some conception of Divine personality by a study of the human, because men are made in the likeness of God; but wherever the endeavour is made to build up the Divine from the suggestion given in man, it must be remembered that the factors of personality in man are finite, while in God they are infinite.

Four things are contained within the realm of personality—Will, Intelligence, Power, and Capacity for Love. A person is a being who can be approached, trusted or doubted, loved or hated, adored or insulted. These essential parts of personality are limited in human beings: the will has its limitations, the intelligence has its limitations, power has its limitations, love has its limitations.

It is not unthinkable that there may be illimitable will, intelligence, power, and love, and that yet the personality shall remain. Neither is it unthinkable that there may be a Being Who can be approached, trusted or doubted, loved or hated, adored or insulted, having all these elements of personality in infinite measure. Granted that in the Divine there are to be found the elements that exist in other rational beings, it is surely not unthinkable that these may be infinite in the Divine, while yet they are finite in man.

The Christian position is that it is perfectly easy to understand that man, within a circumscribed area, is a picture of the Divine; but that yet, by so much as he is circumscribed and limited, he is not himself Divine. In this sense man was made in the image of God; but that of which he is the image is like him, yet unlike him. It is unlike him in the fact that all that is found in man of essential majesty and grandeur in limited degree, is to be found in God Himself unlimited and illimitable. The Holy Spirit, then, is a Person, possessed of Will, Intelligence, Power, and Capacity for Love.

In the third century of the Christian era, Paul of Samosata advanced a theory denying the Divinity of Christ, and regarding the Holy Spirit as an influence, as an exertion of a Divine energy and power. He attempted to finally explain the terms of the New Testament and of Scripture; and in his attempt to say the last definite, formulated word, he found he must cut away certain supernatural mysteries that surrounded the doctrine of God as contained in revelation; and declared that there was no Trinity, that Jesus was not Divine, and that the Spirit was simply the influence moving out from God, the energy of God exerted upon other people. About the time of the Reformation two men, Lælius Socinus, and his nephew Faustus Socinus, revived the theory, and many accepted it.

The growth and decay of what is known as direct Socinianism is not the subject now under consideration. These facts in the history of the Church are mentioned in order that it may be understood whence came the teaching, the influence of which was like leaven, spreading far more widely through the Church than the circle of those who actually called themselves Socinians. This circle of people had a well-defined doctrine to teach. The great mass of Christian people refused to accept the doctrine; but, alas! passed unconsciously under its chilling influence, and unknowingly almost the whole Church came to think of the Spirit of God as an influence, if not to speak of Him as such!

In the Authorized Version the personal pronoun which refers to the Holy Spirit is translated by the neuter *it,* an index of the trend of thought among Christian people. Men prayed of the Spirit as of *it,* an influence, an energy, proving that the Socinian thought had chilled the zeal and the enthusiasm of Christian doctrine concerning the Holy Spirit.

One of the most remarkable signs in the present time of the revival of the truth of the personality of the Spirit, is the reintroduction in the Revised Version of the masculine pronoun wherever the Spirit is referred to. In that apparently simple and insignificant matter there is a clear revelation of the fact that God is calling His people everywhere to a recognition of this most important doctrine of the personality of the Spirit.

A list of the passages containing the references of Jesus to the Holy Spirit in the Synoptic Gospels and in the Gospel of John will be found as a footnote. Let them be carefully perused.[1] There are two lines of teaching which run through these utterances. First, the most solemn warning ever uttered in the hearing of men had reference to the Holy Spirit. In the Gospels of Matthew, Mark, and Luke, Christ affirms that His own words may be rejected, that His own Person may be spoken against, and that these things shall be forgiven to the sons of men; but that they who refuse the teaching of the Spirit can find no forgiveness, because the final apostasy of such, the final turning of the back upon the work and mission of the Spirit, constitutes what our Lord speaks of as *eternal sin. Whosoever shall blaspheme against the Holy Spirit hath never forgiveness, but is guilty of an eternal sin*[2]—a deep, searching, and awful thought. The man who can sin against the Holy Spirit, refusing His teachings, deliberately turning his back upon, and his will against, the message of the Holy Spirit, is in danger of passing into a realm in which his sin is not temporary and transient, but is eternal and abiding. Such were the most awfully solemn words which fell from our Lord's lips. It is not conceivable that a man should sin against a mere influence or energy, so as to bring himself into danger of eternal sin. There is in every word

[1] Matt. x. 19, 20, xii. 28*, 31, 32, xxii. 43, xxviii, 19*. Mark iii. 29, xii. 36, xiii. 11, xvi. 16*. Luke iv. 18*, xi. 13*, xii. 10-12, 49*. xxi. 15, xxiv. 48*. John iii. 3-8*, iv. 10-14*, v. 21*, vii. 37*, vii. 37, 38*, xiv. 16, 17, 26*, xv. 26*, xvi. 7-11, 13-15*, xx. 22*. Acts i. 5, 8*. (* Peculiar to this Gospel.)

[2] Mark iii. 29.

of the warning evidence of an assumption in the mind of Christ of the personality of the Holy Spirit.

The Gospel of John contains Christ's systematic teaching concerning the Holy Spirit. He speaks of Him as the *Paraclete.* This is the title of a Person. It is indeed one of the incommunicable, untranslatable words of Scripture. Neither *Comforter* nor *Advocate* fully expresses its meaning. Both, and even something beyond, would be required to do this. Much would have been gained if no attempt had been made at translation, the word itself becoming the most familiar name of the Spirit.

In these discourses, when speaking of the Paraclete, Jesus does not, in one single instance, use the word which can be construed as indicating thought of the Spirit as an influence. *He shall teach, He shall bear witness, He shall convict, He shall guide.*[1] These activities attributed to the Holy Spirit must be the activities, not of an influence depending upon another and separate will, but the activities of a Person, of One Who unites within His own Being all the essential elements of personality, Will, Intelligence, Power, and Love. Whether in the solemn warnings of the Synoptic Gospels, or in the teachings concerning the mission of the Spirit in the Gospel of John, the fact is most evidently set forth, that in the mind of Christ the Holy Spirit was thought of, not as an influence, an energy

[1] John xiv. 26, xv. 26, xvi. 8, 13.

merely, but as One capable of exercising functions and doing deeds which were impossible to any other than a Person.

Again, the Holy Spirit is not only a Person, but a Divine Person. Another heresy arose in the Church in the fourth century. Arius, a presbyter of Alexandria, taught that God is one eternal Person; that He created a Being infinitely superior to the angels, His only begotten Son; that this only begotten Son of God did in His turn exercise His supernatural power by the creation of a third Person, that third Person being the Holy Spirit.

The difference between Socinianism and Arianism lies in the recognition by the latter of the personality of the Spirit while denying His proper Deity. According to Arius, the Holy Spirit is a Person, a created Person; and if created, then not Creator; and if not Creator, then not Divine. The Nicene Creed was drawn up and adopted as a corrective to this error of Arianism, which had obtained a firm hold in the early Church.

Most assuredly the Scriptures teach not only the personality of the Spirit, but His Divine personality. The unity of two passages in the Old and New Testaments throws light upon this subject.

Then said I, Woe is me! for I am undone; because I am a man of unclean lips, and I dwell in the midst of a people of unclean lips: for mine eyes have seen the King, the Lord of hosts. . . . And He said, Go, and tell this people, Hear ye indeed, but understand not; and see ye indeed, but perceive not.[1]

The prophet had come into the presence of God, and was undone by the vision.

The New Testament contains an exposition of that vision of Isaiah.

And when they agreed not among themselves, they departed, after that Paul had spoken one word, Well spake the Holy Spirit by Isaiah the prophet unto your fathers, saying,

Go thou unto this people, and say,
By hearing ye shall hear, and shall in no wise understand.[2]

Paul declared that it was the Holy Spirit Who uttered the words which Isaiah distinctly says were spoken by the Divine Being. Thus the interpretation of the Old Testament by the New reveals the fact of the Divinity of the Holy Spirit.

A new covenant was promised long before the coming of the Messiah.[3] In the Epistle to the Hebrews the old promise of the covenant of Jehovah is identified with the new dispensation of the Spirit.[4] It is evident that the Persons at first sight apparently different are identical, and that the Spirit spoken of in Hebrews comes in fulfilment of the prophecy uttered by Jeremiah.

[1] Isa. vi. 5. [2] Acts xxviii. 25 26. [3] Jer. xxxi. 31-34. [4] Heb. x. 15-17.

Again, the works attributed to the Holy Spirit must be the works of Divinity.[1] Genesis declares that out of the chaos, cosmos was brought by His brooding and force. In the Gospel of John regeneration is declared to be His work.[2] Paul distinctly states that God will quicken our mortal bodies through the Spirit.[3] Creation, regeneration, resurrection, these are works which can only be brought about by infinite power, and therefore the Spirit is not only a Person, but a Divine Person.

Omnipresence, omniscience, and omnipotence, attributes that appertain only to God, are all attributed to the Spirit.[4]

The Scriptures then teach that the Holy Spirit is a Person, having all the Divine attributes and able to do all Divine works. The mystery is acknowledged, and it is very profound. To finally explain it is impossible; but this impossibility of explanation is to be accounted for by human limitation and by the fact that the finite can never grasp the Infinite. The facts must be reverently accepted as forming an integral and necessary part of the system of revealed religion. To deny the personality of the Spirit, and to deny the Divine personality of the Spirit, must eventuate—as it has done in every system where it has been attempted—in denial of the Divinity of the Son, and in the denial of the

[1] Gen. i. 2. [2] John iii. 5. [3] Rom. viii. 11. [4] Rom. viii. 26, 27. 1 Cor. ii. 10, 11. 1 Cor. xii. 11.

Divinity of the Son there must also be included—as there always has been—a denial of the atoning work of the Son. The doctrines of the Son—His Cross and Passion—and of the Spirit—His personality and Divinity—are closely connected, and one cannot be interfered with without detriment to the other. Denying these truths, the whole fabric of revealed religion breaks down.

III

THE RELATION OF THE SPIRIT TO THE TRINITY

THE doctrine of the Trinity is one of the declared facts of Holy Scripture of which no perfect explanation is possible to minds that are finite. The idea of one Essence subsisting after a threefold manner, and in a Trinity of relationships, finds nothing in the phenomena of nature upon which it can fasten as a sufficient symbol. There have been many attempts to give the mind of man an understanding of this mystery by some such symbol. The mystics attempted, by analogy, to reconcile the doctrine to human reason. They made use of such figures as those of the light, the radiance, and the heat of the sun; the fountain, the flux, and the stream of the river; the root, the stem, and the flower of the plant; the intellect, the will, and the feeling of man; or, perhaps most familiar of all, the human being, consisting of spirit, soul, and body. They declared that in all these things, and indeed throughout nature, there is a perpetual reproduction of that which is the essence of the Divine—Trinity in Unity.

All these illustrations suggest a Trinitarian possibility; but if employed as final symbols, they only serve to mystify. They are insufficient, and differ from the declared facts so radically, that the impression they create, as to the great underlying fact of Divinity—One in Three and Three in One—is vague and evanescent. As in the case of the personality of the Spirit, so here; the things which are evident are faint and incomplete suggestions of the facts concerning the Infinite. The Scriptures contain a progressive revelation of the doctrine; but when the last word has been said, there is no attempt made to explain the mystery. All that they give is a declaration of the fact, without attempting to give that which would be incomprehensible, a definition or explanation that is final.

The first hint of plurality in the unity of the Godhead is found in the words: *And God said, Let Us make man in Our image, after Our likeness.*[1] To claim that as a definite and final statement of the doctrine of Trinity in Unity would be false. It is the privilege of those who live in the light of the New Testament to view the Old Testament therein. *All things were made by Him; and without Him was not anything made that hath been made.*[2] This refers to the work of the Word, the

[1] Gen. i. 26. [2] John i. 3.

eternal Son, in creation. It was by His intermediation that the worlds were formed in the beginning.

Thus the Bible story of creation reflects the presence of the three Persons in the Trinity,—the Father, as original Source; the Son, as Intermediary; the Spirit, as the Medium through which creation came into being.[1]

The truth is still further developed in the words: *So shall they put My name upon the children of Israel.*[2] The emphasis should be laid upon the word *so,—SO shall they put My name upon the children of Israel.* The method indicated is to be found in the three preceding verses.

The Lord bless thee, and keep thee:
The Lord make His face to shine upon thee, and be gracious unto thee:
The Lord lift up His countenance upon thee, and give thee peace.[3]

This is the trinity of benediction in unity, *My name* in threefold repetition. It is not probable that the priest of the old dispensation, in pronouncing that benediction, had a clear understanding of the truth of the Trinity in Unity, but a hint was enshrined therein which prepared the way for future development. Thus in the priestly benediction of Numbers, there is an advance upon the suggestion of Genesis.[4]

[1] Gen. i. 1. John i. 3. Gen. i. 2. [2] Num. vi. 27. [3] Num. vi. 24-26. [4] This priestly benediction of the Old Testament has its fulfilment in that of the New: *The grace of the Lord Jesus Christ,*

The messages of the prophets contain suggestions on the subject: *In the year that King Uzziah died I saw the Lord sitting upon a throne, high and lifted up, and His train filled the temple. Around*[1] *Him stood the seraphim: each one had six wings; with twain he covered his face, and with twain he covered his feet, and with twain he did fly. And one cried unto another, and said, Holy, holy, holy, is the Lord of hosts.*[2]

Isaiah was permitted to have a vision of the King, high and lifted up. He heard the doxology of the hidden place, the cherubim and seraphim chanting the praise of the Eternal, and they sang *Holy, holy, holy, is the Lord of hosts,* a threefold ascription of praise to the one Person.

In this prophecy also is to be found perhaps the most clear statement of the doctrine of the Trinity that the Old Testament contains: *Come ye near unto Me, hear ye this; from the beginning I have not spoken in secret; from the time that it was, there am I: and now the Lord God hath sent Me, and His Spirit.*[3] There is an important alteration in this passage from the Authorized Version, which reads: *The Lord God, and His Spirit, hath sent Me.* The *Me* here is the coming One of Whom the prophets wrote and spoke—the great Deliverer, the Messiah, Jesus. The Authorized Version

and the love of God, and the communion of the Holy Spirit, be with you all. Here also the Trinity is named. 2 Cor. xiii. 14.

[1] *Around, (not above, as in the English Version)* . . .
Dr. G. A. Smith.

[2] Isa. vi. 1-3. [3] Isa. xlviii. 16.

makes it appear as though Christ was sent by God and the Spirit; but in the Scriptures He is never so spoken of. This change in the Revised Version is of the utmost importance; for it contains a prophecy of the coming of Christ and the dawning of the dispensation of the Spirit. *God hath sent Me, and His Spirit.* Here the Trinity is distinctly revealed, not as a doctrine, but incidentally in the midst of prophecy. All that the New Testament unfolds in its beauty is suggested in this prophecy, uttered centuries before the coming of the Messiah—God sending Son and Spirit.

The New Testament takes up the suggestion of the Old, making it clear and plain: *And Jesus, when He was baptized, went up straightway from the water: and lo, the heavens were opened unto Him, and He saw the Spirit of God descending as a dove, and coming upon Him; and lo, a voice out of the heavens, saying, This is My beloved Son, in Whom I am well pleased.*[1] The voice of the Father is heard from the heavens, announcing His pleasure in the Son, while the anointing Spirit descends upon Him. This is a manifestation of the one God in His threefold personality. Thus, at the outset of Christ's public ministry, the truth of the Trinity was declared by a solemn manifestation, though the men around did not then comprehend the deep significance of the event.

The Paschal discourses contain the Lord's full teach-

[1] Matt. iii. 16, 17.

ing on the subject of the Spirit. This is of sufficient importance to demand special attention, and a subsequent chapter will be devoted to it.[1]

One more reference claims attention in this section. The Master having finished His work on Calvary; the Resurrection being accomplished; and the Ascension imminent; He gave to His disciples the commission under which they were to serve. In connection with this, He committed to them the great baptismal formula, which contains the most simple and concise statement of the Trinity that is to be found in the whole of Scripture: *Baptizing them into the name of the Father and of the Son and of the Holy Spirit.*[2] The phrase *of the,* in each case clearly marks the separation of personality, but the singular number of *the name,* by which these are prefaced, marks the unity of the Godhead. That baptismal formula is the consummation of all previous suggestion, and the standard of all subsequent teaching concerning the Trinity.

The declarations of Scripture, then, may be summarized thus:—In one essential Godhead there coexist three Persons, consubstantial, coequal, and coeternal. This mystery cannot be explained nor defined, because it is beyond the grasp of the finite; and no explanation is attempted in the inspired Book.

Accepting the doctrine of the Trinity, it is now competent most reverently to enquire what Scripture

[1] John xiv., xv., xvi. [2] Matt. xxviii. 19.

teaches concerning the relation of the Holy Spirit to the Trinity.

The Holy Spirit is always spoken of as the third Person in the Trinity.

In the historical revelation the last personality revealed is that of the Spirit. That of the Father was the supreme point in the creation and history of the Jewish people: *The Lord our God is one Lord.*[1] Then there came the revelation of the Son; and lastly, as the consummation of His mission, came the revelation of the personality of the Spirit.

Again, in the actual facts of the awe-inspiring mystery of the Trinity, the Holy Spirit is not first.

It is distinctly stated that the Spirit is sent; and Christ declared that the Spirit *proceedeth from the Father.*[2] This order can never be reversed. The Father cannot be spoken of as being sent of the Spirit, neither can He be said to proceed from the Spirit; therefore, in a sense hard to understand, but distinctly announced, the Holy Spirit cannot be the first Person in this mystery of the Trinity.

Nor can He be the second Person therein. The Son is spoken of as sending the Spirit from the Father, and as Himself sending the Spirit.[3] Within the realm of Divinity the Son is never said to be sent by the Spirit. It is said of Jesus that the Spirit drove Him into the wilderness; but that was in

[1] Deut. vi. 4. [2] John xiv. 26, xv. 26. [3] John xv. 26, xvi. 7.

His representative capacity as a Man. In His Divinity He is sent by the Father, for the accomplishment of the Father's work; but He is never spoken of as being sent by the Spirit. Consequently, the Spirit, sent by the Son is the third Person within the Trinity, in the order in which these Persons move in the mighty majesty of their wondrous activities. The great creeds of the Church have caught up the idea of the Spirit proceeding from the Father and from the Son. While there is no direct and positive statement of the kind, still the very argument of the Lord's own teaching, as recorded in the Gospel of John, coincides with that expression of the truth.

The term *third* must be used with most careful limitations. As used with reference to the Persons in the Godhead, it does not imply inferiority. Once in the writings of Paul he reverses the order, and names the Spirit first: *One Spirit, even as also ye were called in one hope of your calling; one Lord, one faith, one baptism, one God and Father of all.*[1] Upon another occasion he changes the order again, and places the Spirit in the second place: *Now I beseech you, brethren, by our Lord Jesus Christ, and by the love of the Spirit, that ye strive together with me in your prayers to God for me.*[2] The word *third* is not used in the sense of inferiority. Perhaps that fact will most surely be understood by remembering that the term *third* has here no reference to

[1] Eph. iv. 4-6. [2] Rom. xv. 30.

time. The time element must be eliminated from all consideration of Divine things. It is very difficult to do this. Speaking of the Father, and of the Spirit proceeding from the Father, unconsciously, but none the less certainly, the time element enters into the conception. It may be argued that there can be no procession save that which has a beginning. If that be true, neither can there be a Source from which procession is made, which has no beginning. When dealing with the things of God, time is not; it finds no place in the boundless Being of the Eternal. The procession of the Spirit from the Father is as eternal as is the Father from Whom the Spirit proceeds.

The relation of the Spirit to the Father is declared in the words: *The Spirit proceedeth from the Father.*[1] He is the gift and outmoving of the Divine Essence, the Eternal Spirit. This defies analysis. It is a truth declared, which remains an impenetrable mystery. Men have no right to make any attempt to discover that which is not revealed. It is the simple declaration of the Word of God, that the Spirit proceedeth from the Father; and there the matter must be left.

The relation of the Spirit to the Son is indicated in the words of Jesus in which He declared that the Son receives from the Father, and the Spirit therefore proceedeth through the Son.[2] Professor Swete, in a paper read before the Church Congress several years ago, in

[1] John xv. 26. [2] John xiv. 16, xv. 26.

well-chosen words stated, with as much clearness as is possible, the great mystery of the Spirit's relationship to the Son. These are his words: *The Son is thus the Intermediary of the self-communication of God. His mediation in creation and in grace rests ultimately on His mediation in the mystery of the Holy Trinity.* The mediation in creation, and the mediation in redemption are based upon the fact, that Scripture declares, that in an inscrutable manner, in a way that defies definition, the Son is intermediary between Father and Spirit, in that great and sublime and magnificent mystery of the Trinity itself.

Here, again, the fact of limitation of language must be borne in mind. These statements refer to eternal attitudes, and consequently they are dateless.

With great reverence and solemnity the question of the function of the Holy Spirit within the Trinity may now be considered.

No such consideration would be possible or proper if it were not based upon the fact that a statement is made with regard thereto in Scripture: *For who among men knoweth the things of a man, save the spirit of the man, which is in him?*[1] This is the apostle's analogy. There immediately follows the statement of a truth of the utmost importance: *Even so the things of God none knoweth, save the Spirit of God.* These words clearly reveal the fact within the mystery of the Trinity—the

[1] 1 Cor. ii. 11.

Spirit is the seat of the Divine consciousness. The eternal Spirit knows the things of the eternal Godhead: *The Spirit searcheth . . . the deep things of God.*[1]

That statement leads to the inner heart of this great mystery; and from it a most important deduction is drawn. Seeing that the Spirit of God is the seat of Divine consciousness, He is also the Spirit of revelation. As it is the Spirit of God Who knows the things of God, it must of necessity be the Spirit Who unveils and reveals those things, as much as is necessary and possible, to those outside the marvellous and mysterious circle of the Deity. In that great fact, beyond perfect comprehension, lies the secret of the inspiration of Scripture, and of the presence and work of the Spirit in the Church and in the world.

If any person should accept this attempt to examine one of the greatest mysteries of our most holy religion, feeling that now all is clear, then the attempt has sadly and awfully failed. This subject must be left where God has left it—a revealed mystery, not the revelation of a mystery. That is to say, revelation has declared a mystery; revelation has not given the explanation of that mystery. The mind of man could never understand, even if the most simple language were used, the Trinity in the Unity of the Godhead, or the relation of the Persons in the Godhead to each other. But, so far as it is necessary and possible for man to see it, *things*

[1] 1 Cor. ii. 10.

which eye saw not, and ear heard not, and which entered not into the heart of man . . . unto us God revealed them through the Spirit.[1]

The statement may thus be made in brief words. There is one God. There are three Persons within the Unity. The Holy Spirit is third in position, for ever proceeding from the Father, through the mediation of the Son. That Holy Spirit is the Consciousness of God, and therefore the Revealer of God.

While these things are too high and too wonderful for perfect exposition, yet, so far as is necessary for redemption and life and final perfecting, God has allowed the light of the glory of the inner facts of His own Being to fall upon the human mind.

[1] 1 Cor. ii. 9, 10.

BOOK II

IDEAL CREATION

Fair are the flowers and the children, but their subtle suggestion is fairer.
Rare is the rose-burst of dawn, but the secret that clasps it is rarer;
Sweet is the exultance of song, but the strain that precedes it is sweeter;
And never was poem yet writ, but the meaning outmaster'd the metre.

Never a daisy that grows, but a mystery guideth the growing;
Never a river that flows, but a majesty sceptres the flowing;
Never a Shakespeare that soar'd, but a stronger than he did enfold him,
Nor ever a prophet foretells, but a mightier seer hath foretold him.

Back of the canvas that throbs, the painter is hinted and hidden;
Into the statue that breathes, the soul of the sculptor is bidden;
Under the joy that is felt, lie the infinite issues of feeling;
Crowning the glory reveal'd, is the glory that crowns the revealing.

Great are the symbols of being, but that which is symboll'd is greater;
Vast the create and beheld, but vaster the inward Creator;
Back of the sound broods the silence, back of the gift stands the giving;
Back of the hand that receives, thrill the sensitive nerves of receiving.

Space is as nothing to Spirit, the deed is outdone by the doing;
The heart of the wooer is warm, but warmer the heart of the wooing;
And up from the pits where these shiver, and up from the heights where those shine,
Twin voices and shadows swim starward, and the essence of life is Divine.

RICHARD REALF.

IV

THE SPIRIT IN CREATION

THE work of the Spirit in creation, and His perpetual presence and manifestation therein, are subjects full of fascination, and yet strangely neglected. So much attention has been given to the work of the Spirit in its regenerative aspect, that His generative activities have been in a large measure overlooked. The origin and the preservation of everything in nature are spiritual.

No lily-muffled hum of a summer bee
But finds some coupling with the spinning stars;
No pebble at your foot but proves a sphere,
No chaffinch but implies the cherubim.
. . . . Earth's cramm'd with heaven,
And every common bush afire with God;
But only he who sees takes off his shoes—
The rest sit round it and pluck blackberries.[1]

The sacred Writings abound in statements with regard to this aspect of the Spirit's work.

What magnificent figures are contained in the words of the Psalmist!

[1] Mrs. E. B. Browning.

He bowed the heavens also, and came down;
And thick darkness was under His feet.
And He rode upon a cherub, and did fly:
Yea, He flew swiftly upon the wings of the wind.
He made darkness His hiding-place, His pavilion round about Him;
Darkness of waters, thick clouds of the skies.
At the brightness before Him His thick clouds passed,
Hailstones and coals of fire.[1]

It is evident, from a careful reading of this Psalm, that it is a declaration of the perpetual presence of God in all such manifestations. Wherever thick darkness is, it is under the feet of God; whenever the wind passes with swift impetuosity, He flies upon the wings thereof; wherever darkness is, it is God's hiding-place, a pavilion round about Him; whenever the darkness is dispersed, it is before the brightness of His rising. In every gleam of the glory of nature there is the evidence of an ever-present God.

The final words of that great doxology which Isaiah heard from the inner temple are of great interest in this connection:[2] *In the year that King Uzziah died I saw the Lord sitting upon a throne, high and lifted up, and His train filled the temple. Around*[3] *Him stood the seraphim: each one had six wings; with twain he covered his face, and with twain he covered his feet, and*

[1] Ps. xviii. 9-12. [2] Isa. vi. 1-3. [3] See footnote, p. 29.

with twain he did fly. And one cried unto another, and said, Holy, holy, holy, is the Lord of hosts: the whole earth is full of His glory. The uplifted Lord is the centre of adoration in the courts of heaven; but not there only is His splendour seen—*the whole earth is full of His glory.*

A marvellous declaration of the fact of the presence of God in all nature is to be found also in the great Theophany of the Book of Job.[1]

For the purposes of this study, however, it will be sufficient to consider certain definite statements of Scripture, in which the work of the Holy Spirit in creation is clearly set forth in varied aspects.

First compare the earliest reference to the Spirit with one in the prophecy of Isaiah:—

And the earth was waste and void; and darkness was upon the face of the deep: and the Spirit of God moved upon [or as the margin gives it, *was brooding upon*] *the face of the waters.*[2]

But the pelican and the porcupine shall possess it; and the owl and the raven shall dwell therein: and He shall stretch over it the line of confusion, and the plummet of emptiness.[3]

Exactly the same Hebrew words are used in each case to describe the desolation. The word translated *waste* in Genesis is translated *confusion* in Isaiah; the word translated *void* in the one case is translated *emptiness* in

[1] Job xli., xlii. [2] Gen. i. 2. [3] Isa. xxxiv. 11.

the other. This comparison throws light upon the story of creation.

The first picture is that of the Spirit brooding over chaos. Science agrees that the earth must have been in such a condition as this before the appearance of man. How this condition of things arose, whether through some mighty catastrophe whelming a previous order, or through the omnific word of God, no man can tell; both science and revelation are silent. These opening words of the Book of Genesis introduce this planet while yet waste and void, and declare that, for the accomplishment of the change from this condition to that of order, the Spirit brooded over the face of the waters. He acted as the Administrator of the will of God, as expressed by the word of God. The will of God is that order should supersede disorder. The Word of God announces that will, beginning with the first utterance: *Let there be light.*[1] By the brooding of the Spirit over the chaos the light came. That is the unvarying order of the activity of God in creation.

This is not an account of the first creation of matter. Concerning that, man has no definite knowledge.

In the beginning God created the heaven and the earth.

And the earth was waste and void.[2]

How long the interval between these verses no man can tell. Scripture makes no announcement thereupon,

[1] Gen. i. 3. [2] Gen. i. 1, 2.

and the declarations of science are but surmises. But when the present order was established, it was by the Spirit of God brooding upon confusion and emptiness, as the Power through which the Divine will was realized. The earth as it is to-day is therefore the direct outcome of the action of the Holy Spirit.

Another of the Psalms is full of suggestiveness:—

By the word of the Lord were the heavens made;
And all the host of them by the breath of His mouth.[1]

The word *breath* here might with perfect correctness be written with a capital letter—*the Breath of God's mouth.* Here again is revealed the will of Jehovah, uttered by the Word of Jehovah, and accomplished by *the Breath of His mouth;* but the sweep of thought is greater than before. It is not a description of the bringing of order to one small planet, but the record in a sentence of the creation of the heavens and all the host of them. The phrase includes all the myriad wonders of the universe around. By the Word of God, and by the Breath of His mouth, came the systems of which man is just beginning to learn that in their entirety they are undiscoverable. The point at which astronomical science has now arrived is an acknowledgment, that beyond the utmost reach of anything which can be studied through the agency of the telescope, lie illimitable space and innumerable worlds.

This has been forcefully stated by Dr. Pierson in his

[1] Ps. xxxiii. 6.

Many Infallible Proofs, and the whole paragraph is of such a nature that it is here inserted at length:—

The fact of the vast host of stars is a fact of modern discovery. Hipparchus, about a century and a half before Christ, gave the number of stars as 1,022, *and Ptolemy, in the beginning of the second century of the Christian era, could find but* 1,026. *We may on a clear night, with the unaided eye, see only* 1,160, *or, if we could survey the whole celestial sphere, about* 3,000. *But when the telescope began to be pointed to the heavens, less than three centuries ago, by Galileo, then for the first time men began to know that Jeremiah was right when he made the stars as countless as the sand on the sea-shore. When Lord Rosse's instrument turned its great mirror to the sky, lo, the number of visible stars increased to nearly* 400,000,000! *and Herschel compares the multitude of them to glittering dust scattered on the black background of the heavens. When John Herschel, at the foot of the dark continent, resolves the nebulæ into suns, and Lord Rosse, as with the eye of a Titan, finds in the cloudy scarf about Orion " a gorgeous bed of stars," and the very Milky Way itself proves to be simply a grand procession of stars absolutely without number—how true is the exclamation of Jeremiah,* 600 *years before Christ,* 2,200 *years before Galileo; " The host of heaven cannot be numbered!"*[1] *Who taught Jeremiah astronomy?*

[1] Jer. xxxiii. 22.

All these unnumbered hosts were made by *the Word of the Lord and the Breath of His mouth.*

Take now one of the passages in the Book of Job. The words are those of the patriarch himself:—

By His Spirit the heavens are garnished;
His hand hath pierced the swift serpent.[1]

The meaning of the passage is obscure, but light is thrown upon it by the context:—

He stirreth up the sea with His power,
And by His understanding He smiteth through Rahab.[2]

That is a perfect picture, in miniature, of a storm-swept sea, over which the dark clouds hang dismally. Then follow the words: *By His Spirit the heavens are garnished.* It is a vision of the bringing back of the blue and the light to the heavens, after the sweeping of a storm; and in this strange expression, *His hand hath pierced the swift serpent,* Job borrows one of the Eastern nature-myths, in illustration of the fact that the calm which follows the storm in nature is—actually and symbolically—the work of the Spirit of God. Job was in fact, or in imagination, looking out upon a storm-tossed sea; he saw it suddenly calmed, the clouds dispersed, and the heavens garnished with beauty. The reference to the flying serpent is difficult of understanding. One says that the reference is to the sign of the zodiac; another that it describes the long train of the

[1] Job xxvi. 13. [2] Job xxvi. 12.

cloud, as the wind of the Spirit disperses and drives it away; and yet another that the term has reference to the whole arch of heaven, as pierced by the hand of God. Between these views it is not possible to decide, but certainly it is a figure of speech, most probably indicating the driving away of the storm-clouds like trailing serpents, as the heavens smile in sunlight after the storm is spent. The main statement is, however, perfectly clear—that the transformation of beauty is wrought by the Spirit of God.

Another interesting statement is found in the prophecy of Isaiah concerning the agency of the Spirit in nature: *The grass withereth, the flower fadeth; because the Breath of the Lord bloweth upon it.*[1] This declaration is at first sight almost staggering. That the Spirit of God comes as a genial summer zephyr upon nature is easy to understand; but it is difficult to believe that He comes also as the fierce blast of God. Yet it is certainly true. He brings death as a process, and a necessity. The pitiless east wind has in it the breath of health. Let there be no more east wind, no more north-east wind, no more biting, keen blast of death, and what would become of nature? Surely Kingsley entered into the spirit of this when he sang:—

Welcome, wild North-easter!
Shame it is to see
Odes to every zephyr,
Ne'er a verse to thee.

[1] Isa. xl. 7.

Through the black fir forest
Thunder harsh and dry,
Scattering down the snowflakes
Off the curdled sky.

Come; and strong within us
Stir the Viking's blood,
Bracing brain and sinew;
Blow, thou wind of God.

When the east wind blows, and the flowers are nipped, and the blade of grass is curled and shrivelled almost as if by the blast of heat, then the Spirit of God is sweeping the ground and preparing for the springing of life in response to the kiss of His gentler wind.

In close sequence consider the words:—

Thou sendest forth Thy Spirit, they are created;
And Thou renewest the face of the ground.[1]

That which follows the death-wind of the Spirit is His life-wind. The first is Winter; the second is Spring. Nothing ever finds its way to Spring save through Winter. The budding of life and the flowers that blossom upon the sod in Spring-time are the result of the cold east wind that swept the hills and the valleys during Winter days. These are not mere figures of speech. The cold and icy wind blows under the direction of the Spirit of God; and the wind which kisses earth, and makes it smile in flowers, is the messenger of the self-same Spirit.

The prophecy of Ezekiel opens with a magnificent

[1] Ps. civ. 30.

piece of imagery, of which no final nor exhaustive exposition is here attempted. There is, however, no more gorgeous vision of the glory of God to be found in the whole of His Book. To Ezekiel, the bard and prophet, there was granted a vision of that glory in the great chariot of Divine movement and life. The vision embraced the creatures of the earth, and the appearances of the heavens. The colours of earth and of heaven were seen. Beryl is translucent and green as earth and sea; sapphire is blue, as of the highest heavens; and over the amber glory in that vision was the appearance as of a Man occupying the highest position. The wheels that turned and went, and the wings that beat the air, were symbolic of the presence of God in every form of nature. *Whithersoever the Spirit was to go, they went; thither was the Spirit to go: and the wheels were lifted up beside them; for the Spirit of life was in the wheels.*[1] Ezekiel was looking at God, so far as man may gaze upon Him. He was beholding the vehicle of the Divine movement, and found that it takes earth and heaven to manifest it. Whether it be in the machinery, the procession, the regular motion of earthly things, or whether it be in the unapproachable and unexplainable light and splendour of the upper world, God is everywhere. Earth's living creatures and heaven's splendours move by the Spirit of God. This is a most inadequate analysis of the vision of that chapter, but it is sufficient to in-

[1] Ezek. i, 20 (margin).

dicate the central truth thereof—that every movement of the wheels of nature, every beat of the wing of created thing, is by the impulse and energy of the Spirit of life.

From the study of these passages it is evident that, as by the power of the Spirit cosmos was produced out of chaos, so by the ever present and active power of the Spirit in the processes of nature cosmos is maintained.

There is yet one more phase of this subject suggested by the apostle Paul: *For the earnest expectation of the creation waiteth for the revealing of the sons of God. For the creation*[1] *was subjected to vanity, not of its own will, but by reason of Him Who subjected it, in hope that the creation itself also shall be delivered from the bondage of corruption.*[2] Paul had no narrow conception of his Master's work. He saw the regenerative work of Jesus, as administered by the Spirit, passing out, not merely into human lives, but into the whole creation.

We know that the whole creation groaneth and travaileth in pain together until now.[3]

We ourselves groan within ourselves.[4]

The Spirit Himself maketh intercession for us with groanings which cannot be uttered.[5]

[1] The change from *creature* of the Authorized to *creation* of the Revised is important. The former word may suggest an individual, the latter embraces all created things.

[2] Rom. viii. 19-21. [3] Rom. viii. 22. [4] Rom. viii. 23. [5] Rom. viii. 26.

A trinity of agony is here revealed,—nature groaning and travailing in pain; the child of God groaning and waiting for deliverance; and, most wonderful of all, the Spirit of God making intercession with groanings which cannot be uttered.

Thus it is declared that the Spirit is present in creation, and all through creation as a regenerative Force; and ere the work of the Cross of Christ be completed on this planet, every inch of it will be renewed. The whole creation that to-day *groaneth and travaileth in pain together* will feel the balm, the healing, and the blessing of the work of Christ. Trees and flowers will again realize what they also in some sense have lost by the fall of man. *All the trees of the field shall clap their hands. Instead of the thorn shall come up the fir tree, and instead of the brier shall come up the myrtle tree: and it shall be to the Lord for a name.*[1] The Spirit Who created, preserves, energizes, and moves through all nature, is in nature as an intercessory Force—as a Force administering, by processes which are beyond analysis, the great work of the Christ Himself; and this ministry will eventuate in the removal of the curse from nature, and its consequent renewal, glorious and perfect.

From these seven scriptures certain deductions may be made.

The Holy Spirit is the Director of all order in creation. He is first seen brooding over the primal chaos,

[1] Isa. lv. 12, 13.

and producing order. He is for evermore the Intelligence and Force of all mathematical precision in nature. The old words are still true: *Seedtime and harvest, and cold and heat, and summer and winter, and day and night shall not cease.*[1] These processions follow with infinite precision, and mathematical regularity, by the direction of the Holy Spirit of God. It is by no mere fortuitous accident that morning succeeds upon night, and that day sinks and nestles into the bosom of darkness. These things follow because there is an ever-present Spirit of intelligence, the Spirit of the living God, at work to the utmost bound of created things.

The Holy Spirit is the Creator of beauty. He is revealed in the garnishing of the heavens, in the blue of day, and in the darkness of night with all the splendours of stars scattered in profusion across it. All these are beautiful, and they appeal to the beautiful in man; for they were born of God, as man is born of God. Not only is this true of the beauty which overawes, but also of the form of every leaf and flower and spire of grass. The stately sweep of the sea and the delicate dome of the dew-drop are alike the outworking of the wisdom and energy of the Spirit of God. Man, born of the Spirit, in the grace of transformed life gives evidence of the Spirit's power. So also, in different degree and kind, but none the less certainly, is it with the flowers of the field. Put them under microscopic test,

[1] Gen. viii. 22.

and their exquisiteness and beauty and precision and regularity reveal the working of the Spirit of God. He in nature not only directs the order, but creates the varied and varying beauty.

Again, the Spirit is the Breath of renewal. Through death He ever leads to life. That fact is revealed even in the death of the Son of God, for it is written that *through the eternal Spirit* He *offered Himself without blemish unto God.*[1] The Winter wind that beat upon Him in His dying was but the preface to the Summer wind of Pentecost.

These things are to be seen everywhere in nature because the self-same Spirit Who works in regeneration works also in generation. This Spirit, the Breath of renewal through death, comes with manifold glory in the Spring, bringing a renewal of the earth. Winter's cold precedes Spring. Autumn's fire precedes Winter's cold. Through fire and cold the Spirit ever moves to new life; and the new forms of beauty, manifold and wondrous, with which the face of the earth is renewed are His.

To those who live and walk in the Spirit, all creation is seen to be of God. No man can find God through nature; but every man may find nature through God. If man begin with nature, he cannot climb from it to God; but if he begin with God, he may enter into the mystic region, wherein lies true appreciation of the glo-

[1] Heb. ix. 14.

ries and beauties of nature. No man has ever yet seen or understood the beauty of the daisy, save as he has seen that the floweret, blossoming and blooming to-day, to be trodden underfoot to-morrow, is a part of the work of the same Spirit which is transforming human character and life. The Spirit of God brooded over the chaos and brought forth the cosmos. The Spirit of God has, for evermore, been brooding over nature; and every form of beauty, and every form of order, and every manifestation of renewal are parts of the Divine expression of Himself. All creation is of God, to the man who lives and walks with Him.

One Spirit—His
Who wore the platted thorn with bleeding brows
Rules universal nature! Not a flower
But shows some touch, in freckle, streak, or stain,
Of His unrivall'd pencil. He inspires
Their balmy odours, and imparts their hues,
And bathes their eyes with nectar; and includes,
In grains as countless as the sea-side sands,
The forms with which He sprinkles all the earth.
Happy who walks with Him, whom what he finds
Of flavour or of scent in fruit or flower,
Or what he views of beautiful or grand
In nature, from the broad majestic oak
To the green blade that twinkles in the sun,
Prompts with remembrance of a present God.

V

THE SPIRIT IN RELATION TO UNFALLEN MAN

A TOO constant contemplation of man as he is, has resulted in failure to appreciate his original condition. Man to-day, even at his best, does not realize the full Divine intention. The whole race is suffering from the sin of the past; limitation is to be found everywhere; yet man has endeavoured to build up out of the broken fragments of the Divine ideal, an ideal for himself.

In the answer to the Psalmist's question,

What is man, that Thou art mindful of him?
And the son of man, that Thou visitest him?[1]

the terms in which man is spoken of are not those of limitation, but those which reveal the perfection of the Divine ideal.

For Thou hast made him but little lower than God,
And crownest him with glory and honour.
Thou madest him to have dominion over the works of Thy hands;

[1] Ps. viii. 4-6.

Thou hast put all things under his feet:
All sheep and oxen,
Yea, and the beasts of the field;
The fowl of the air, and the fish of the sea,
Whatsoever passeth through the paths of the seas.[1]

That picture is not fulfilled in the experience of any human being in the present times. There is little about man to suggest that he is but little lower than God—little of the crowning with glory and honour that the Psalmist speaks of; and man has in a large measure lost his dominion. The animal creation is tamed in part; but by far the greater part of it is outside the dominion and the authority of man. The writer of the Letter to the Hebrews claims a partial fulfilment of that ideal of man in the Person of Jesus Christ. He claims the ultimate fulfilment of the whole ideal in the Person and through the work of Christ; but he shows that the larger fulfilment waits for a while. After quoting the Psalm, he proceeds to say: *But now we see not yet all things subjected to Him. But we behold Him Who hath been made a little lower than the angels, even Jesus, because of the suffering of death crowned with glory and honour.*[2] He declares that in the Person of Christ, two of the notes of ideal manhood have been realized: first, *made a little lower than the angels;* secondly, *crowned with glory and honour.* But he has already said, *We see not yet all things subjected to Him*—much lies in the

[1] Ps. viii. 7, 8. [2] Heb. ii. 8, 9.

future for fulfilment; but this claiming of the fulfilment of the ideal of the Psalm in the Person of Christ suggests a line of consideration which it is profitable to follow. God's ideal Man and the relation the Spirit of God bears to that Man is discovered by a study of the Person of Christ.

The present enquiry, then, bears upon the ministry of the Spirit in the life of unfallen and ideal man. The consideration is necessarily limited to two examples —Adam and Jesus. The first is valuable in one respect only, as it reveals the essential glory of the creation of man. The life of Adam is not chronicled in detail; and there is therefore no certain knowledge of its character or duration. The relation existing between God's perfect man and the Holy Spirit can only be understood by a study of the life of Jesus.

There are two scriptures which lead into the very heart of the study.

Many persons have a great difficulty about the second account of creation as given in the Book of Genesis.[1] After the apparent completion of the story, at the close of the first chapter, there is a repetition in the second; and a casual observer may imagine that there is not merely repetition, but contradiction. As a matter of fact there is none. The second story is the complement of the first; it is the unfolding of a certain aspect of creation about which nothing was declared in the first.

[1] Gen. ii. 7.

That reveals three facts:—

i. That man was a result of counsel in the Godhead: *Let us make man.*[1]

ii. That he was created *in the image of God.*[2]

iii. That he was given dominion over a previous creation.

In the subsequent story there is an unfolding of his nature. Man is now shown as uniting in his own person the material with the spiritual, the earth with the heavens, the things that perish and pass with the things that abide for ever. God made man of the dust of the earth—a material basis—and breathed into him the breath of lives, thus creating a spiritual being. Through that inbreathing by God, the conscious side of man's nature was born, and he *became a living soul.*[3]

The dust which was of the earth was devoid of self-consciousness. Man's power to enter into his new environment, his power to submit to the government under which he was placed, his power to enter into the new companionship, which completed the possibilities of his being—all these were the result of the inbreathing of the Breath of lives by God. Man is not man, apart from the direct ministry and sustaining power of the Spirit of God. Everything that man is, in the essential facts of his being—everything which differentiates between a man and an animal—is due to this peculiar form of inbreathing, whereby man became a conscious soul.

[1] Gen. i. 26. [2] Gen. i. 27. [3] Gen. ii. 7.

In the illumination of the Breath of God man entered upon a perfect environment. The Garden had been planted by God; the earth had been created by God. Everything that surrounded man, in the moment of his generation, had been prepared by Divine wisdom and infinite tenderness. This being amid the Garden—looking upon the glory of its trees, its plants, its flowers, and all its varied life, comprehending and understanding the whole—is man; and in his powers of comprehension he is distinguished from all lower forms of being, and therein lies his chief glory. He entered thus into the beauty and the glory of his environment, by virtue of the fact that there had been breathed into him the Breath of lives. He was the offspring of God.

In Him was life; and the life was the light of men.[1] The first meaning of this statement is that the living Word of God, the eternal Christ, is the Centre and Source of all life. But it also suggests that in man life was different from life anywhere else; in man life became light. There was life in the plant, and life in the lower animals; but when God inbreathed to man the Breath of lives, He bestowed a life in which lay the element of light. In man, creation first looked back into the face of God, and knew Him. No lower form of life knows God. In every flower which decks the sod, there is present the touch of God; but no flower knows it. In all life there are present the power and energy of

[1] John i. 4.

God; all things live and move and have their being in Him; but apart from man, none are conscious of it. In man life became light, consciousness, knowingness. Man was created to look back into the face of God, and to know Him, to understand in some measure the mystery of His being. Man entered into the perfect environment of the Garden, knew it, appreciated it, and discovered God in it, because there had been inbreathed to him the Breath of lives.

Not only was this inbreathing of light upon his environment; it was, moreover, understanding for his occupation. He was to have dominion over the lower animals, to dress and to keep the Garden. He was able to do this through the inbreathing of the Spirit of life. The energy and the light for wise dominion were the energy and the light of God. The guidance necessary for the further development of the wonderful creation of the earth was provided by the inbreathing of that self-same Spirit.

Man entered not only upon perfect environment, with perfect and sufficient occupation, but he also came under perfect government. *The Lord God commanded the man*[1] is the statement which marks the Divine sovereignty. Man understood and obeyed the law in the energy of that inbreathing of the Breath of life.

Not only did he enter into environment, occupation, and government, but also into companionship. God

[1] Gen. ii. 16.

made woman to be his companion. He entered into that new relation which created and conditioned the whole social range of human life in the power of that same Breath of lives. When man is thus viewed from the standpoint of original intention as seen in the picture of Edenic beauty and power, it is evident that the natural is spiritual and the spiritual is natural, and that there is no single aspect of human life which is not under the government of the inspiring Spirit of God. Every part of man, the fact of his being, his power to touch his environment with appreciation, his power to follow a daily occupation, his power to submit to government, his power of social relationship and companionship—all are made possible of highest realization by the great inbreathing of God, the work of the Spirit, whereby man becomes *a living soul.*[1]

These are some of the suggestions of the glory of man, gathered from the creation story. They are no more than suggestions, because the story of sin follows quickly thereupon.

Passing over the intervening centuries, as contributing no perfect example of man, the daybreak of the race was reached in the advent of the second Man, Jesus. He was the final and perfect example of ideal human life. *In Him was life; and the life was the light of men.*[2] That is not only a declaration that life becomes light in men; it also claims that the life which is light in

[1] Gen. ii. 7. [2] John i. 4.

man had its most perfect outshining in the Person and character of Christ. It may be said of the Incarnate Word—In Him was life; and His life was the light of men. To know what human life is, He must be known. To have seen Him as the disciples saw Him, was to have seen the perfection of human life in every one of its aspects. In His physical appearance, in His mental life, in His spiritual nature, He was a perfect unveiling of the glory of ideal Manhood.

The art of the great masters seems to have been dominated by a conception of the physical appearance of Jesus which was utterly false. He is represented as pale, thin, wan, emaciated. Perhaps Hoffmann alone has discovered the glory of the beautiful Christ, perfect in form and comeliness, perfect in beauty. Truly it is written of Him that *His visage was so marred more than any man,*[1] but it was the marring of beauty, not of ugliness nor decrepitude. The marks of anguish were evident upon His face, and the lines of sorrow ploughed deeply into it; but when the young ruler met Him, fell before Him, and said *Good Master,*[2] the exclamation was most probably drawn from him by an overwhelming sense of the beauty and the majesty of the appearance of Christ. Before the surging sorrows of His public ministry rolled over His heart, there is very little room for doubt that He was the most perfectly lovely Man the world had ever gazed upon. Any other

[1] Isa. lii. 14. [2] Mark x. 17.

conception of Christ dishonours Him. In Him was life, and in Him the life was light; so that men might know, by looking at the Christ, all the beauty and all the glory of the Divine ideal.

This applies also to His mental culture. A sinless soul, living in communion with nature, would understand her to an extent which must be impossible for the sinful one, who attempted to grasp her inner teaching merely on the lines of ordinary study. The men of the synagogue said of Christ, when, after absence from Nazareth, He returned and talked with them: *How knoweth this Man letters, having never learned?*[1] The emphasis of their question lay, not upon the spiritual teaching of Christ, but upon the illustrations He used, and upon His evident acquaintance with what was then spoken of as learning. It was not that they were overwhelmed by a sense of His spiritual insight; for, then as now, men knew that spiritual insight often belonged to those who had no learning. They were impressed by the beauty of His expression, the wealth of His illustration, and His evident familiarity with those things, to become acquainted with which, men gave themselves up to long courses of study. The mind of Christ was refined, cultured, and beautiful—not through the ordinary process by which limitation and sin endeavour to overcome their deficiencies, but by a pure response to a perfect ideal, and by the inspiring touch and revelation of the Spirit of God.

[1] John vii. 15.

The relation which existed between this perfect Man of the Gospels and the Spirit, was of the closest. Christ's very existence as a Man was due to the miraculous power of the Holy Spirit. The whole of His perfect Being, spirit, soul, and body, was the creation of the Spirit of God. Therefore, every action of that body, every relation of the body to the mind, and of the mind to the spirit, all the inter-relations of His complex nature, were balanced within the spiritual Power that created them, and were conditioned for evermore by the suggestions, impulses, and energy of that Power.

As Christ passed through childhood and the earlier years of His life, and into those of His mature manhood, all were directed by the Spirit of God. Luke, writing of the time when He went down with His parents from the presentation in the Temple, declares that *He advanced in wisdom and stature, and in favour with God and men.*[1] Afterwards, in the course of His public ministry, Jesus said, *Which of you by being anxious can add one cubit unto his stature.*[2] Applying the philosophy of His teaching to His own growth, the fact is clear that His physical growth was the outcome of submission to Divine law, revealed by the inspiration of the Spirit. It is also chronicled that He went down from the Temple with His parents, and was subject to them. That subjection being over, He came forth into public ministry, and with scathing, scorching denunciation testified against the men who excused themselves from caring

[1] Luke ii. 52. [2] Matt. vi. 27.

for the needs of their parents, on the plea that their goods were Corban, or gifts devoted to God. He was angry with them because their action was contrary to Divine law. Subjection to His parents on His part had been a perpetual answer to a perpetual law, written in His heart by the finger of the Spirit of God, as He passed through His boyhood.

How perfectly He was devoted to the law of God as it had been given to His people! He studied it, meditated in it, and became so familiar with it, that when His public ministry began, He knew exactly what it had to teach. In obedience to that law He went up to His Jewish confirmation at the age of twelve, and took His place among the doctors, not, as it is so often represented, as a rude, precocious boy, trying to puzzle old men, but as a sweet boy-disciple, answering their questions with a lucidity which astonished them, and asking them, out of the working of His own pure mind, questions which were amazing, coming from One so youthful. When He returned to Nazareth, He took up the tools of His reputed father's craft, and mastered their use. Through long years He abode in that shop, working out the will of God, and revealing in every piece of carpentry the design and beauty and force of the inspiring Spirit, by Whom He was created and for evermore sustained.

As the week drew to a close, and the Sabbath came, He went *as His custom was*[1] to the place of prayer, to

[1] Luke iv. 16.

worship God among His people, with His face toward Jerusalem.

All His life, in both its earlier years and maturer manhood, was conditioned in and by the Spirit, to Whose guidance and direction He never gave one single moment's slight.

Turning from these earlier years to the account of His public ministry, Matthew, Mark, Luke, and John give the story of His anointing with the Spirit for the duties of that ministry. Immediately after the Anointing came the Temptation. Matthew, Mark, and Luke alike chronicle the fact that He was taken to that Temptation by the Spirit of God. When the Temptation was over, He entered upon the years spent for the most part before the gaze of the multitudes. Luke declares that He went to that ministry in the power of the Spirit. He wrought miracles during those three years; and in his sermon in the house of Cornelius, Peter declared that these also were performed through the presence with Him of the Holy Spirit: *Jesus of Nazareth, how that God anointed Him with the Holy Spirit and with power: Who went about doing good, and healing all that were oppressed of the devil; for God was with Him.*[1]

When at last the years of public ministry were ended, and He went to the exodus of the Cross, He accomplished that in the same power, for He *through the eternal Spirit offered Himself without blemish unto God.*[2]

[1] Acts x. 38. [2] Heb. ix. 14.

After the sojourn in the shades of darkness He rose again, as Peter declared, through the power and energy of the Spirit.[1] Between His resurrection and ascension He sojourned for a while among His disciples; and during those days He taught them, organized them, gave them their definite instructions, and this He also did through the Holy Spirit, as Luke declared in the opening statements of his second treatise: *The former treatise I made, O Theophilus, concerning all that Jesus began both to do and to teach, until the day in which He was received up, after that He had given commandment through the Holy Spirit unto the apostles whom He had chosen.*[2]

The story of the perfect Man of nineteen hundred years ago is the story of a human life, perpetually inspired and energized by the Holy Spirit of God. From birth, through growth, testing, and ministry, on to death and resurrection and the organizing of the apostolate, the whole is a perpetual and unbroken harmony—a harmony created by the moving of the Wind, the Spirit of God, upon the instrument of a perfect human being.

From the glimpse of glory in the first creation, it was evident that creation was of the Spirit; and that the power by which man enters into a perfect environment and occupation, and submits to a perfect government, and continues in the joy of a perfect companionship, is

[1] 1 Pet. iii. 18. [2] Acts i. 1, 2.

the power of the Breath of lives. This is finally proved by the unfolding of the ideal in the life of Jesus of Nazareth. To know, then, what perfect humanity is, Christ must be known.

Every man's being, in all its complex wonders, exists by the creative energy of the Holy Spirit.

The expressions often used by Paul, *the natural man* and *the spiritual man,* were constantly placed in antithesis. He taught that the natural cannot comprehend the spiritual. A theologian's expressions must be understood in the sense in which he uses them, before his theology can be understood; and this is as true of Paul as of any other theologian. Whenever he spoke of the natural man, he intended to refer to man in the condition resulting from the sin of the race; and therefore, in the higher heights of vision, and in the larger, truer outlook upon humanity, he spoke on such occasions, not of the natural, but of the unnatural. Sin is not natural to man. Men are *shapen in iniquity,* and *go astray as soon as they be born, speaking lies;*[1] but the reason for this is that something unnatural has been introduced, which has poisoned every successive generation. The work of the natural Man Jesus is to restore unnatural things to the spiritual, which is the truly natural. No man has discovered the possibilities of his own being, no man understands the glory of his own life, until he has come to see that all he has within himself is of God,

[1] Ps. li. 5, lviii. 3.

save the taint of sin, which has no right to be there, and for the putting away of which the perfect One went into the darkness of His Passion-baptism.

The full and proper use of all the powers of man is made in the energy of the Holy Spirit; and physical health lies within that realm. Here it is necessary to safeguard the position held, even at the cost of repetition. The subject of which this chapter treats is that of ideal man. Under the present order of disciplinary life, sickness is a veritable ministry of infinite love, not only for the sake of those who suffer, but of others, who through their suffering learn more of God; but the man who abides in the will of God, obeys the law of God, trusts himself wholly to the inspiration of the Spirit of God, that man will touch higher physical conditions than are possible to him apart from such living. That man cannot be compared with another man, because there are many different sets of laws to be considered in any such comparisons; but he may be compared with himself, and, doing this, it may assuredly be declared that, abiding within the realm of the Divine law, his life submitted to the law of the Divine Spirit, he will touch, by such submission and abiding, a higher realm of physical force and power than by any other law of life in which it is possible for him to live.

So also in the mental sphere. Everything that is pure and beautiful in poetry, art, music, and science is the direct outcome of the revealing Spirit of God. Men sometimes affirm that Shakespeare was inspired; and they are right,—by no means in the same sense in which the Bible is; but he was inspired nevertheless, and that by the Holy Spirit of God. All pure genius is inspired —not in the same degree as the Scriptures, because not for the same purpose, but by the same Person. All the heights of vision granted to the strong, pure poet, are created for his seeing. Wordsworth, for instance, because he was pure in heart, saw God. All mental magnificence that is pure is an inspiration of the Spirit of God. There may be a prostitution of a Divine gift in this realm also; and a man upon whom God has bestowed the gift of vision, may abuse that gift, and debase it to the purposes of hell. The power to see, whether it be exercised in poetry, art, music, or research, is not born of evil, but is the child of heaven, the flaming, glorious proof of the touch of the Spirit of God upon the mind of man.

Given a man redeemed, regenerated, and wholly possessed by the Spirit, that man has the fullest entrance into all true life. The Divine ideal for man is that he should be spiritual, and that his spirituality should be realized by the surcharging of his whole being with the Spirit of God. That Spirit will turn all the forces of his life into the one direction of true worship. He will employ every power for that purpose for which it was created, and enable a man to worship in the beauty of holiness perpetually. In work and rest, through pathos and humour, by laughter and tears, will be shown, through the Spirit, the glories of creation; and thus God will be glorified in the full life of man.

How far even Christian people are as yet from the realization of this ideal! Toward this the Spirit is working; and at the last there shall not be merely the two men out of all the years as examples of the ideal, but a regenerated humanity, brought into the presence of God by the work of the Saviour and of the Spirit, without spot or wrinkle or any such thing.

BOOK III

THE SPIRIT PRIOR TO PENTECOST

Through storm and sun the age draws on
  When heaven and earth shall meet,
For the Lord has said that glorious
  He will make the place of His feet.
And the grass may die on the summer hills,
  The flower fade by the river,
But our God is the same through endless years.
  And His word shall stand for ever.

What of the night, O watchman,
  Set to mark the dawn of day?
The wind blows fair from the morning star,
  And the shadows flee away.
Dark are the vales, but the mountains glow
  As the light its splendour flings,
And the Sun of Righteousness comes up
  With healing in His wings.

Shine on, shine on, O blessed Sun,
  Through all the round of heaven,
Till the darkest vale and the farthest isle
  Full to Thy light are given—
Till the desert and the wilderness
  As Sharon's plain shall be,
And the love of the Lord shall fill the earth
  As the waters fill the sea.

Sunday Afternoon Verses.
(W. ROBERTSON NICOLL)

VI

THE WORK OF THE SPIRIT FROM THE FALL TO THE MESSIAH

BY an act of wilful rebellion man distanced himself from God, and was alienated from the life of God.[1] The grace of the Divine heart immediately announced a reconciliation. No sooner was sin committed than there was declared the purpose of grace and love, not in detail and in fulness, but in a promise that came to be understood more fully as the ages rolled. Speaking to the enemy, God said: *It shall bruise thy head, and thou shalt bruise His heel.*[2] Necessarily the process of that reconciliation have been slow, and even yet are not fully and finally accomplished. The Divine love outran in its utterance the actual accomplishment of its purposes. All the arrangements of the old dispensation for the approach of man to God by way of sacrifice were based upon the coming sacrifice of Jesus Christ. The blood of bulls and of goats and the ashes of a heifer never took sin away; but they did help men, amid the twilight

[1] Eph. iv. 18. [2] Gen. iii. 15.

in which they lived and worshipped, to understand the principle of sacrifice, without which there could be no remission of sins. In the plan of God, the Lamb slain was the way of reconciliation; and although the Son of His love could not be manifested until *the fulness of the time,*[1] yet for the sake of man, and in the purpose of God, the Lamb was slain *from the foundation of the world.*[2]

The glorious announcement of New Testament ministry is contained in the words, *God was in Christ reconciling the world unto Himself;*[3] but He was so in purpose, long before the historical fact was accomplished, upon which the larger, fuller dispensation should depend.

The Fatherhood of God was a fact before the coming of Jesus. He illuminated it for men, so that since His coming they have understood it as never before. Though men had wandered and lost their sense of relationship, God was ever their Father, and His presence their home. Even in those old days, before the full light of the glory of God had shone upon man's pathway in the face of the Christ, there were souls who discovered the fact of the Fatherhood, and passed their days homed in God. The same law of procedure is discoverable also with reference to the work of the Holy Spirit.

The whole being of man was conditioned in the energy and the wisdom of that Spirit. The knowledge

[1] Gal. iv. 4. [2] Rev. xiii. 8. [3] 2 Cor. v. 19.

of this fact man had lost by reason of his sin; and the Spirit, resisted, was separated from the actualities of human life. From the moment of the Fall a new form of His ministry began, which was partial, occasional, special, and prophetic of the great dispensation to be ushered in, when the true light of sacrifice had made plain the way for the clearer apprehension of Fatherhood.

The present age is pre-eminently the dispensation of the Holy Spirit, in which He has a specific work, differing from that of preceding ages. This work is based upon the work of Christ, and was impossible until He had finished that work and ascended on high.

It must, however, be remembered that in the past the Spirit had not a constant ministry. The differences between then and now are most clearly defined. Until after the death, resurrection, and ascension of Christ, the Spirit is not spoken of as creating a Church by His own abiding indwelling. Neither is He spoken of as the one direct and only Administrator of the affairs of such a body. And yet again, He is not spoken of as a Sanctifier. All the other aspects of the Spirit's work are found—not continually and perpetually, and in an abiding sense, as they are to-day, but as special occasions demanded.

There is also this important distinction between the old, and new dispensations. In the old, the Spirit came upon and filled men for specific work without reference to character. In the new, after the accomplishment of the work of the Cross, this is never so. His filling for service always depends upon His application of the work of the Saviour for cleansing and holiness.

Certain phrases of Old Testament Scripture reveal both the methods and character of the Spirit's work during those long centuries.

He is spoken of as coming upon men, as coming mightily upon men, as abiding in men, and as filling certain men for specific work.

There may be a great many subdivisions of the eighty-eight passages in which the Holy Spirit is directly mentioned in the Old Testament;[1] but, broadly stated, the method of the Spirit is marked by these four statements. It is not stated that He came upon, nor that He came mightily upon the whole nation; nor, again, is it affirmed that He abode in or filled the whole nation. In that fact lies the difference between the old dispensation and the new. At Pentecost the Spirit came upon all, He came mightily upon all, He came to abide in all, He came to fill all. There may be many members of the Church of Jesus Christ who have not realized in their own experience all this fourfold work of the Spirit; but that is not to be laid to the charge of the economy of grace, but rather to the failure of such persons to realize the purpose of God.

[1] Dr. Elder Cumming, in his book *Through the Eternal Spirit* has compiled a catena of passages in which the Holy Spirit is directly mentioned in the Bible. In the Old Testament there are eighty-eight passages in all.

The Spirit fell upon Gideon. He had in his own home and family broken down the altar of Baal, in order that he might make a protest against idolatry; and after he had done this *the Spirit came upon him.*[1]

David was doubtful as to the loyalty of Benjamin and Judah. *Then the Spirit came upon Amasai,*[2] and he spoke words which convinced David of the loyalty of these tribes.

Zechariah, the son of Jehoiada the priest, was raised up to protest against idolatry in the holy places; and, in order that he might do it, *the Spirit of God came upon him.*[3]

Upon these three men the Spirit came for very different reasons: upon Gideon, after he had broken down the altar of Baal, and in order that he might become the leader of the people to victory; upon Amasai, in order that the loyalty of two tribes might be believed by the king; upon Zechariah, in order that he might utter a protest against idolatry.

The same thought lies within each—*the Spirit came upon them.* The Hebrew word literally means that the Spirit clothed Himself with them—not that the Spirit fell upon them as an anointing, but the Spirit took hold of them, passed into them, and made them the instruments through which He accomplished His work. The thought conveyed to the mind of the Hebrew reader is, that the Spirit clothed Himself with Gideon, the Spirit clothed Himself with Amasai, the Spirit clothed Himself

[1] Judg. vi. 34. [2] 1 Chron. xii. 18. [3] 2 Chron. xxiv. 20.

with Zechariah. Here there is a revelation of one of the methods of the Spirit under that dispensation. For the doing of a special work, for the delivery of a special message, for the announcement of the immediate purpose of God, the Spirit clothed Himself with a man, and the Divine energy moved out in speech and in deed; so that through the man was known the will of God, and seen the power of God. These are three instances out of many in which men became the clothing of the Spirit. The distinction must be observed: it was not that these men were clothed with the Spirit, but that the Spirit clothed Himself with them for the doing of specific work.

Take the second thought. The Spirit of God *came mightily upon*[1] Samson, and he slew a lion. Saul joined a company of the prophets; the *Spirit of God came mightily upon him, and he prophesied.*[2] Samuel poured the anointing oil upon David, and the Spirit *came mightily upon* him.[3]

In these cases an entirely different word is used. It is not said that the Spirit clothed Himself with them, but that the Spirit came upon them; and the thought is that of forcing forward, or pushing. The literal meaning of the word is, that the Spirit attacked these men, came upon them with compulsion, forced them forward to a certain activity. Under the compulsion of the Spirit, Samson slew the lion, Saul joined the prophets

[1] Judg. xiv. 6. [2] 1 Sam. x. 10. [3] 1 Sam. xvi. 13.

and uttered words of prophecy, and David went forward to the work of governing the people. How different is the manifestation of the power!—the slaying of a lion, the uttering of the truth of God, and the governing of the people; but in each case the action was under the impulse of the same Spirit.

There are two passages in the Old Testament where it is said that the Spirit dwelt in men. Pharaoh said that in Joseph there dwelt the Spirit of God, and that therefore he was discreet and wise.[1] When a successor to Moses was needed for the government and leading of the people, Joshua was chosen because in him dwelt the Spirit of God.[2]

Whether Pharaoh understood his own expression may be very doubtful, but it is certainly worthy of note that in each of the cases cited, the Spirit of God created fitness for government; and this fitness consisted, not in autocratic, tyrannous power, but in discretion, wisdom, gentleness, and beauty of demeanour. Such were the manifestations of the indwelling of the Spirit in these men under the old covenant.

Once again, the Spirit filled certain men; and that expression is only used in connection with the work of the making of the Tabernacle. The Spirit of God filled Bezalel that he might have cunning *to work in gold, and in silver, and in brass, and in cutting of stones for setting, and in carving of wood, to work in all manner*

[1] Gen. xli. 38, 39. [2] Num. xxvii. 18.

of workmanship.[1] Thus the whole of the work of the Tabernacle, in its exquisite perfection and in its glorious beauty, was the outshining of the wisdom of the Holy Spirit. No man was glorified in that upreared Tabernacle. Perhaps it was otherwise in the times of decadence; but men of spiritual intelligence, who in the early days looked upon the work of the Tabernacle, would not say, *See how cunning a workman was Bezalel,* but rather, *See how wondrously the Spirit of God has wrought through Bezalel, in the accomplishment of the Divine purpose.*

These illustrations go to show that the Holy Spirit was always interested in and working among men; that He did not abide with them, but that, for special purposes and at special points in their history, He equipped them for whatever the particular moment demanded.

As to the character of the Spirit's work through all these years, there is a wonderful development of revelation concerning the ministry of the Spirit, discoverable in the character of His work as time proceeded: *And it came to pass, when men began to multiply on the face of the ground, and daughters were born unto them, that the sons of God saw the daughters of men that they were fair; and they took them wives of all that they chose.*[2] There were two distinct ideals of life upon the earth, embodied in the seed of Adam through Cain and through Seth respectively, the seventh generation of the

[1] Exod. xxxi. 4, 5. [2] Gen. vi. 1, 2.

one culminating in Lamech, the man who, having committed murder, composed poetry in defence of his sin; and the seventh generation of the other culminating in Enoch, a man of whom it is written that he *walked with God.*[1] Much speculation has been rife concerning the intermarriage of the sons of God and the daughters of men. The exposition of the passage that is most probably correct, is that which treats this intermarriage, as having taken place between people who were godly and those who were godless—between the descendants of Seth and those of Cain. Be that as it may, the condition of things upon the earth had reached a point which is revealed in the words: *My Spirit shall not strive with man for ever, for that he also is flesh.*[2] This is, moreover, a revelation of the work of the Spirit of God in the years from the Fall to the Flood. He was striving with men, convicting them of sin.

Then followed another manifestation of the Spirit in history. The chosen people were being organized for the embodiment of a Divine purpose, and as the medium of a Divine revelation; and the Spirit came upon certain men for the carrying out of all the details necessary to the perfecting of the organization. Then, again, in the passages referred to, concerning Samson, Saul, and David, the Spirit of God is seen manifesting Himself as a Spirit of strength. A period of conflict had come in the history of the chosen people, a race of heroes was

[1] Gen. v. 22. [2] Gen. vi. 3.

needed for the accomplishment of Divine purposes among the nations, and deeds of daring that characterized the period were wrought in the power of the Spirit. Men were raised up to do these deeds of heroism by the Spirit falling mightily upon them.

The prophetic books yield yet another manifestation of the presence and work of the Spirit, and that a most interesting one. Both in Isaiah and in Ezekiel there are fifteen distinct references to the Holy Spirit, which for the most part can only have their fulfilment in the present dispensation or in one which is yet to come. Those days were characterized by the failure of kings and priests to fulfil their several vocations. The kings had become entangled with the idol worship of their heathen neighbours; the priests, smitten with the leprosy of the same unfaithfulness, had been superseded by the prophets. These men, devoted only to the will of God, found nothing amid the decadence of the time to satisfy their hearts and minister to their spiritual well-being. But they were men of vision; and beyond the clouds and the mists they saw the gleam of another day, and they foretold the coming of the Spirit in plenitude and in power. An instance of these foretellings is the prophecy of Joel, which Peter quoted upon the Day of Pentecost, to emphasize the historic value of what men saw passing around them. Amid the darkness and the gloom which had fallen upon the nation, the Spirit of God became the Spirit of hope; so that the essential principles of life were not forgotten.

The Spirit of God was the Spirit of conviction while sin worked itself out from Fall to Flood; He was a Spirit of detailed service while the people of God were being organized into a nationality; He was a Spirit of strength while the people were fighting for the land, and were casting out those who had deeply sinned; and He became a Spirit of hope when the peculiar people had passed into a condition of apostasy and wandering. He lit the horizon with the glow of approaching day. He spoke to ears that listened, and revealed to eyes that gazed; and thus, though they did not perfectly understand, men had some dim foreshadowing of the glories of these days of fulness of spiritual power.

Such is a very rapid summary of the work of the Spirit in that whole period from the Fall to the Messiah.[1]

No clear view of present-day aspects of the Spirit's ministry is possible apart from a just and clear conception of His place in history. The Spirit Who brooded over chaos, and Who breathed into nature the life which blushes and blooms into beauty in every branch and leaf and flower—that same Spirit has always been interested in the affairs of men. There is, however, a very distinct difference between the method of His work in those bygone days, and the method of His work to-day. In

[1] A small booklet by my beloved and lamented friend the Rev. G. H. C. Macgregor, M.A., entitled *Things of the Spirit*, contains the whole of the passages bearing upon this subject, and thus affords a valuable aid to a careful study of the story of the presence of the Spirit of God among men from the Fall to the days of Jesus.

those days there was no Church. To speak of the Israelitish nation as a Church in the sense in which that word is used to-day is to show no true understanding of what the Church really is. Consequently there was no direct, present, actual demonstration of the Spirit to the nation. Most wonderful of all, Old Testament times knew nothing of the Holy Spirit as the Sanctifier of individual lives, in the New Testament sense of cleansing and keeping. Of course Old Testament saints might have sung as truthfully as the saints of the new covenant:—

And every virtue we possess,
And every victory won,
And every thought of holiness,
Are His alone.

The measure of His work, however, was very different; and the sanctification which embodies all virtue, ensures perpetual victory, and subjects every thought to the obedience of Christ, which is holiness, was unknown. These wonderful manifestations of His power were reserved for the present dispensation. It is full of delightful interest to trace the work of the Spirit through the centuries, preparing the way for the coming of the Christ, until the great moment came which was the fulness of the time. Over all the movements of men the Spirit brooded still, coming as a Spirit of conviction of sin, and as a Spirit of special wisdom for definite service, and yet again as a Spirit of strength for conflict, and continually as a Spirit of hope amid decadence. Thus the things of God were made known amid men, in the measure necessary and possible, by that Spirit of God, Who, within the mystery of the Deity, is the Consciousness of God, and the Revealer of that Deity to man.

VII

THE SPIRIT DURING THE MISSION OF THE MESSIAH

DURING the days of Israel's decay the Spirit, through the prophets, had spoken of the coming One. Hope had been preserved in the heart of the nation through the visions of future glory contained in the wonderful words that had been uttered by the messengers of the King. Even these voices had been silent for nearly four hundred years, from the days of Malachi to those of John the Baptist. During that period, however, a small remnant had kept the hope of Israel brightly burning, by loyalty to the principles of government which had been so often declared.

At last the long silence was broken by John, who announced the advent of One Whose distinguishing work should be that of baptizing men with the Holy Spirit and with fire. To the vast crowds that gathered upon the banks of the Jordan he said: *I indeed baptize you with water; but there cometh He that is mightier than I, the latchet of Whose shoes I am not worthy to unloose: He shall baptize you with the Holy Spirit and with fire.*[1] As the Spirit bore a close relation to Jesus as perfect and unfallen Man, so also did He to the office and work of the Messiah. At the commencement of His ministry the Lord claimed as His own the sacred anointing of the Holy Spirit for the fulfilment of His mission:—

The Spirit of the Lord is upon Me,
Because He anointed Me to preach good tidings to the poor:
He hath sent Me to proclaim release to the captives,
And recovering of sight to the blind,
To set at liberty them that are bruised,
To proclaim the acceptable year of the Lord. . . .

And He began to say unto them, To-day hath this scripture been fulfilled in your ears.[2]

The Spirit brooded over the chaos of old, the power of God in creation; the Spirit had been present through all the history of the race, coming specially upon men, for special purposes as God willed. Now that the new dispensation was to be ushered in, and the new order initiated, as the Master began that work which He has not yet completed, but towards the completion of which He is still working, He claimed that the Spirit rested upon Him, as the anointing for His mission. The Lord's view of His own mission is revealed in this quotation. He is anointed

[1] Luke iii. 16. [2] Luke iv. 18, 19, 21.

To preach good tidings to the poor:
To proclaim release to the captives,
And recovering of sight to the blind,
To set at liberty them that are bruised,
To proclaim the acceptable year of the Lord.

Standing in the synagogue, reading the words of the prophet, claiming their fulfilment in His own Person, He initiated that new age described by the prophet as *the acceptable year of the Lord.*

The whole of this preparatory work of Jesus Christ was accomplished under the guidance and in the power of the Spirit. The anointing took place at His baptism: *Now it came to pass, when all the people were baptized, that, Jesus also having been baptized, and praying, the heaven was opened, and the Holy Spirit descended in a bodily form, as a dove, upon Him, and a voice came out of heaven, Thou art My beloved Son; in Thee I am well pleased.*[1]

Immediately afterwards He was led by the Spirit in the Temptation experiences: *And Jesus, full of the Holy Spirit, returned from the Jordan, and was led by the Spirit in the wilderness.*[2]

Following this, He entered upon His public work in the power of the Spirit: *And Jesus returned in the power of the Spirit into Galilee.*[3]

There is a clearly marked sequence here. Anointed by the Spirit, full of the Spirit, led by the Spirit, in the

[1] Luke iii. 21, 22. [2] Luke iv. 1. [3] Luke iv. 14.

power of the Spirit—thus He entered upon the specific work of His Messiahship.

During the exercise of that Messiahship He uttered words to His disciples upon one occasion which demand special attention: *If ye then, being evil, know how to give good gifts unto your children, how much more shall your heavenly Father give the Holy Spirit to them that ask Him?*[1] If it were possible to occupy the actual position of the men who heard these words, it would also be possible to understand how startling a statement it was. They knew what the Scriptures of the Old Testament had to teach about the Holy Spirit. They thought of Him as coming on special men for special work, by the direct giving of God apart from human seeking. The thought of asking for the Spirit was absolutely foreign to the whole economy of the past. The circumstances under which Jesus made this statement must be carefully noted. The disciples had watched Him at prayer, and, being attracted by something in His attitude or appearance, said to Him: *Lord, teach us to pray.*[2] He immediately gave them a perfect pattern known as the Lord's Prayer, but more correctly spoken of as the disciples' prayer. He then proceeded to teach them, by analogy, how that God was always waiting to answer importunate prayer. He used a contrast to teach the truth, showing how a friend who is unwilling to rise from rest to supply the necessity of

[1] Luke xi. 13. [2] Luke xi. 1.

another will do so if that other be importunate enough and continue his asking. He summed up the whole thought of importunate prayer in those words that pulsate with meaning: *Ask—seek—knock.*[1]

He then led them along another line of thought concerning prayer; and using the relationship of a father to a child as illustration, He declared God's willingness to give the best gifts to men: *If ye then, being evil, know how to give good gifts unto your children, how much more shall your heavenly Father give the Holy Spirit to them that ask Him?*[2] Their request to be taught how to pray resulted in their hearing the most startling announcement concerning spiritual matters that had ever fallen upon their ears. They were told that if they asked of God with importunity, and understanding that God would give good gifts only, then they might have the Holy Spirit.

This statement must have so staggered these men as to surprise them almost into inaction; for it is evident that they never asked for the Spirit, and therefore never received Him in answer to their own asking. This text is perpetually quoted as having a present-day application. This is due to a failure to draw the line of distinction between the various phases of the Master's mission. The words were spoken to a handful of Jewish disciples gathered around the Jewish Messiah. He was unveiling to them a great secret in all God's deal-

[1] Luke xi. 9. [2] Luke xi. 13.

ings with men—that God would give the Holy Spirit to men who asked, if they did so according to the law of prayer laid down. There is not, however, any evidence that they ever had the Holy Spirit, until that Spirit came along another line of communication. Before the Master left them He said: *I will make request of the Father, and He shall give you another Comforter. . . the Spirit of truth.*[1]

On the previous occasion He had said in effect, *Ask, and ye shall receive the Spirit;* but they did not ask, and did not receive. They never truly saw Christ, nor understood His mission, nor entered into the deep underlying secrets of His life, until after the Spirit had come upon them in answer to His asking. Our Lord here revealed to them the will of God, the attitude of the Divine heart, the preparedness of the Father to bestow the wondrous gift of the Holy Spirit upon them, but there is no evidence whatever that they ever asked or ever received in answer to their own asking.

One of the most difficult passages to translate, perhaps, in the whole of the Gospel of Luke is the one which reads: *I came to cast fire upon the earth; and what will I, if it is already kindled? But I have a baptism to be baptized with; and how am I straitened till it be accomplished!*[2] The *if* marks the sigh of desire. A paraphrase of the passage may contribute to its elucidation: *I came to cast fire upon the earth; and what will*

[1] John xiv. 16 (margin). [2] Luke xii. 49, 50.

I? Would that it were already kindled! The old acceptation of the verse is most incorrect: *I came to cast fire upon the earth; and what will I, if already I find that fire kindled?* The passage is a soliloquy? Jesus turned from teaching His disciples, and it seems as though He lifted His eyes and looked out upon the necessities of men, and said: *I came to cast fire upon the earth; and what will I? If it were already kindled!* or, *Would that it were already kindled!* Then He proceeded: *I have a baptism to be baptized with; and how am I straitened till it be accomplished!* As though He had said it was impossible for Him to cast this fire, as He desired, until He had Himself passed through the baptism that awaited Him.

This scattering of fire refers to the baptism of the Holy Spirit which John had already predicted: *I indeed baptize you with water; but there cometh He that is mightier than I, the latchet of Whose shoes I am not worthy to unloose: He shall baptize you with the Holy Spirit and with fire.*[1]

In the Acts of the Apostles is chronicled the Master's own reference after His Resurrection to that statement of John: *John indeed baptized with water; but ye shall be baptized with the Holy Spirit not many days hence.*[2]

In connection with the baptism of the Spirit at Pentecost it is recorded: *There appeared unto them tongues parting asunder, like as of fire; and it sat upon each one*

[1] Luke iii. 16. [2] Acts i. 5.

of them.[1] Fire was the symbol of the Spirit, purifying and energizing. Jesus took up the thought of John: John baptized with water, He with fire.

In the light of these passages, it is evident that the fire referred to is that of the Spirit which Christ was waiting to scatter upon the earth, and He declared that until His Passion-baptism was accomplished He was unable to fulfil this purpose.

Jesus, anointed by the Spirit, led by the Spirit, full of the Spirit, was waiting to communicate to other men that fulness which resided in Himself, but He was unable to do this until the Cross was an accomplished fact.

That reveals the character of the years of our Lord's ministry. He was laying foundations, laying them deep and strong, upon the righteousness of God in His own life; He was preparing for the tremendous transactions of the Day of Pentecost, and for all that should follow therefrom. Filled with the Spirit, led by the Spirit, He looked upon men with eyes all lit by tender love, and longed to communicate to them this gift of an indwelling Spirit, yet was unable to scatter the fire until His atoning work was done.

During these years of public life our Lord gave teaching concerning the Holy Spirit which has only been thoroughly understood and valued since He passed through the gateway of death into the larger life beyond. All that it is necessary for men to know about the opera-

[1] Acts ii. 3.

tion of the Spirit in this dispensation Jesus Christ Himself declared; and this teaching occupied a most important place in His ministry. It is found wholly within the Gospel of John,[1] and may be divided into two parts —that which is indirect and suggestive, and that which is direct and positive. The indirect and suggestive teaching of Jesus fell from His lips upon different occasions—once to the woman of Samaria, once to a company of Jews, once to the crowds of people who thronged the streets at the Feast of Tabernacles. The direct teaching of Jesus was given, to His disciples only, in the Paschal discourses. These were the last utterances of Christ to them, and contain a perfect statement concerning the work of the Spirit.

In the indirect teaching of Christ, the first instance is that of His conversation with the woman of Samaria: *Jesus answered and said unto her, Every one that drinketh of this water shall thirst again: but whosoever drinketh of the water that I shall give him shall never thirst; but the water that I shall give him shall become in him a well of water springing up unto eternal*

[1] Every reference made in this chapter—and this is not an accident, it is the result of careful analysis of the whole teaching of Christ—is taken from the writings of Luke or of John. There is scarcely anything recorded by Matthew or Mark of the relation of the Spirit to Christ in His work. Matthew views Christ purely as a Jewish Messiah, and necessarily omits the glory of the larger outlook. Mark views Him as a Servant, and sees Him stripped of all supernatural power; but Luke, the Gospel of the universal Saviour, and John, the Gospel of a Divine Lord and Master, contain the revelation of the secret forces that made His ministry.

life.[1] The woman had no clear understanding of the depth of that message, nor had those who heard it from her lips. In common with other words of Christ, it has only come to be understood in the light of the Spirit's dispensation. The water which He gives is the living water of the Spirit, perpetually springing up in the soul of man unto eternal life.

Another statement is contained in a discourse to the Jews directed against materialistic conceptions of communion with God. He declared that it is only in the realm of the spiritual that this communion can be maintained: *I am the Bread of life: he that cometh to Me shall not hunger, and he that believeth on Me shall never thirst.*[2]

The third and last was uttered on the great day of the feast, and is a beautiful statement concerning the ministry of the Spirit and the relation of man to that ministry: *Now on the last day, the great day of the feast, Jesus stood and cried, saying, If any man thirst, let him come unto Me, and drink. He that believeth on Me, as the Scripture hath said, out of his belly shall flow rivers of living water.*[3] Then follows John's inspired exposition of those words: *But this spake He of the Spirit, which they that believed on Him were to receive: for the Spirit was not yet given; because Jesus was not yet glorified.*[4]

[1] John iv. 13, 14. [2] John vi. 35. [3] John vii. 37, 38. [4] John vii. 39.

For this He was preparing by doing a work which would arrest the attention of men and call for their faith; and He declared that men responding to that demand, and exercising faith in Himself, should enter into a new region of life, in which their own personal thirst should be quenched, and out of them flow rivers of living water. All this is condensed truth about the Spirit, uttered by Christ during His life, and only fully understood in the light of subsequent events.

The Paschal discourses are too important to be dismissed hurriedly, and therefore will be considered in following chapters. It will be sufficient here to state their nature. The One of Whom the Spirit was to speak, spoke of the Spirit, by the Spirit. The Spirit's mission is to unfold the glories of the Christ; and men know this to be the case, because the Christ unfolded the glory of the Spirit. There is the most wonderful communion between Son and Spirit revealed in this teaching.

The last point of importance in this connection is the prophetic breathing of the Spirit upon men by Jesus Christ: *Jesus therefore said to them again, Peace be unto you: as the Father hath sent Me, even so send I you. And when He had said this, He breathed on them, and saith unto them, Receive ye the Holy Spirit: whose soever sins ye forgive, they are forgiven unto them; whose soever sins ye retain, they are retained.*[1]

[1] John xx. 21-23.

The place these words occupied in the work of Jesus must be considered, if they are rightly to be understood. He had risen; the Passion-baptism was over. He could no longer say: *I have a baptism to be baptized with: and how am I straitened!* He had been baptized with that baptism, He was no longer straitened in the same sense, but He had not yet ascended into the presence of God. Not until He had actually taken His place in the heavenlies, in the double right of life and death, standing for Himself in the power of a perfect life, and for us in the power of an atoning death—not until He had represented men in the presence-chamber of the King, could He shed forth that great gift of fire which He had come to scatter upon them.

The former treatise I made, O Theophilus, concerning all that Jesus began both to do and to teach, until the day in which He was received up, after that He had given commandment through the Holy Spirit unto the apostles whom He had chosen.[1] For forty days He tarried, giving them commandments, and it is very wonderful to notice that the risen Christ worked in the energy of the Spirit. He gave these men their commandments through the Holy Spirit; and, among other things, He stood in their midst and breathed upon them. The explanation of that act is to be found in what He said immediately before: *As the Father hath sent Me, even so send I you. And when He had said this, He*

[1] Acts i. 1, 2.

breathed on them. He declared the law of continuity of service, that these men were to pick up the threads of the work that He had Himself been doing, and were to weave them into warp and woof, until the whole perfect fabric should be completed. *As the Father hath sent Me, even so send I you.*[1] He had been sent anointed with the Spirit; and now He breathed on His disciples, and said: *Receive ye the Holy Spirit.—As the Father hath sent Me, even so send I you.* He had been sent by the Father in the power of the Spirit, and He sent them in the power of that self-same Spirit.

That this breathing of Christ was a prophetic act is proved by the subsequent facts. Before He ascended He told them that they were not to go, but to tarry until they were endued with power from on high. It was a prophetic breathing. His Passion-baptism was over; He stood among His followers—the little band chosen to carry on His victories and do His work; and, looking at them, He said: *As the Father hath sent Me, even so send I you. . . . Receive ye the Holy Spirit.*[2] It was a typical act, suggesting the power in which they were to go to the work He committed to them.

The whole subject may thus be summarized. The day of new power and of new light was prepared by the ministry of the Son of God and the Son of Man. The light and the glory of the Gospel were created in the mysterious energy, suffering, and agony of the life

[1] John xx. 22, 21. [2] John xx. 21, 22.

of the God-man. The Spirit Who brooded over the chaos, Who had visited men, Who had always been interested in men, and Who had ever carried out the work of God among men, came upon Christ, dwelt in Him, energized Him, and prepared, in His Person, for a larger dispensation. Through His life the Spirit prepared for that death of mystery, as the result of which the Spirit should pass into the life of men, for pardon, purity, and power.

BOOK IV

THE TEACHING OF CHRIST CONCERNING THE SPIRIT

Weary and sad and sorrow-spent were they
In that still upper room,
While the rich crimson of the closing day
Was fading into gloom;
And over all, benumbing soul and sense,
Hung the cold shadow of a dread suspense.

The promise of a Spirit yet to come,
That other Paraclete,
To lead them on to Truth's eternal home
And guide their wandering feet;
They could not soothe the anguish of their heart,
They ask'd in sadness, *Must their Lord depart?*

Yes, after all, or clear and open speech,
Or sayings dark and dim,
They yet had much to learn and He to teach,
Ere they could rest in Him,
Ere they could preach His words with cleansèd lips,
Or He impart His full Apocalypse.

E. H. Plumptre.

VIII

THE COMING OF THE SPIRIT

THE little group of men who had followed the Lord during the years of His public ministry gathered about Him at the Paschal board. Judas had left the company. The others were filled with sadness. It is not necessary to attempt an analysis of their sorrow. Probably there was a great deal of selfishness mixed with it; but there is selfishness in all sorrow, save that which is under the constraint of the Holy Spirit. The shadow of approaching separation fell upon them. The Master administered comfort to their hearts. He told them that He was going away, but they were not to be left comfortless, or, as the word really is, orphans. This statement He explained by unfolding for them the great principles of the new dispensation of the Holy Spirit. He gave them a system of teaching on the coming, character, and mission of the Spirit, with the results following—a system which is clear, concise, and sufficient.

His first statement concerning the coming of the

Spirit[1] is contained in the words: *And I will pray the Father, and He shall give you another Comforter, that He may be with you for ever.*[2] The Holy Spirit is to be the gift of the Father through the Son.

The marginal reading in the Revised Version is, *I will make request of the Father;* but neither rendering perfectly conveys the thought that underlies the word that Jesus used. The conversation of Martha with Jesus, when Lazarus lay dead, throws light on this word: *And even now I know that, whatsoever Thou shalt ask of God, God will give Thee.*[3] Martha used a word for prayer, the word translated *ask,* which Jesus constantly used when speaking of the prayers of other persons, but never of His own prayers. It is a word that conveys the idea of asking as a beggar, as a pauper; and that is how men always pray. The word translated *pray* here is a special one, never used about prayer except in the Gospel of John, and always in that Gospel concerning the prayers of Jesus Christ. This reveals the fact that the prayers of Christ differed from those of other persons. The word suggests, not the petition of some one that asks for something as a favour, but the petition of one who is on a perfect equality with the person to whom it is presented. The thought has within it the idea of perfect fellowship. Perhaps that is better conveyed by the translation: *I will enquire of the Fa-*

[1] In this section, by *the coming of the Spirit,* His advent on the Day of Pentecost to usher in a dispensation is referred to.

[2] John xiv. 16. [3] John xi. 22.

ther, and He shall give you another Comforter.[1] This is by no means a perfect translation, but it approximates more closely to the intention of the original word than either of the other phrases. Christ declared that He was going to the Father, and that He would enquire of, in the sense of holding converse or having fellowship with the Father, and, as the direct result, the Father would send them the Holy Spirit. Jesus, the Jewish Messiah, had said to His disciples: *If ye then, being evil, know how to give good gifts unto your children, how much more shall your Father which is in heaven give good things to them that ask Him?*[2] That was a purely dispensational and Jewish statement; and the men never asked and never received. Now that the Master was leaving them, He said to them: *I will ask, I will enquire of, I will pray the Father, and He shall give you.*

Immediately these great discourses were ended, Christ moved into a higher realm, that of intercession; and John records His words in the presence of God for His people. In that prayer the Lord did not mention the Holy Spirit. The reason for this is to be found in the fact that the prayer for the Holy Spirit could not be offered until His Passion was an accomplished fact. He could not ask for the Spirit save upon the basis of a perfect fellowship, based upon a finished work, until—no longer straitened—He should stand in the presence

[1] John xiv. 16. [2] Matt. vii. 11.

of God. Then, in response to the presence in the highest place of the One Who had accomplished the work, God would give.

The teaching then, of this first statement of Christ, concerning the coming of the Spirit, is that the Spirit is the gift of the Father, through the Son, upon the basis of His finished work. In that lies one point of difference between this dispensation and all that have preceded it. The Spirit came upon men in the past for specific purposes, at special seasons; but the Son of His love passed into the presence of God, having accomplished the Divine purpose, and upon the basis of that finished work the Spirit was poured out.

Concerning the Spirit's coming, the Master also said: *These things have I spoken unto you, while yet abiding with you. But the Comforter, even the Holy Spirit, Whom the Father will send in My name, He shall teach you all things.*[1] This reveals that the Spirit is to be the Messenger of the Father in the name of the Son.

Of His own coming Jesus said, *I am come in My Father's name,* and, *I told you, and ye believe not: the works that I do in My Father's name, these bear witness of Me.*[2] Upon two occasions He distinctly stated that He came and worked in His Father's name, that the name of God was the sphere of His work. Now He declared: *The Holy Spirit, Whom the Father will send in My name, He shall teach you all things.* As the Son

[1] John xiv. 25, 26. [2] John v. 43: x. 25.

came in the name of the Father, and as the name of the Father was the sphere of the work of the Son, so the Spirit was to come in the name of the Son, and the name of the Son was to be the sphere of the Spirit's work. This is perfect continuity.

A third statement on this subject is contained in the words: *But when the Comforter is come, Whom I will send unto you from the Father.*[1] This declares the Spirit to be the Messenger of the Son, from the Father.

This reference can only be understood by looking at its context: *He that hateth Me hateth My Father also. If I had not done among them the works which none other did, they had not had sin: but now have they both seen and hated both Me and My Father. But this cometh to pass, that the word may be fulfilled that is written in their law, They hated Me without a cause. But when the Comforter is come, Whom I will send unto you from the Father, even the Spirit of truth, which proceedeth from the Father, He shall bear witness of Me.*[2] Jesus had lived among men, unknown, misunderstood—men had hated Him; and now the Spirit was to be sent by the Son, as from the Father, in vindication of the character, ministry, and mission of the Son.

Yet one other declaration follows: *Nevertheless I tell you the truth; It is expedient for you that I go away: for if I go not away, the Comforter will not come unto you; but if I go, I will send Him unto you.*[3] Thus the

[1] John xv. 26. [2] John xv. 23-26. [3] John xvi. 7.

Spirit is directly the Messenger and Gift of the Son. He will Himself send the Spirit to His disciples upon the basis of His union with the Father, a union consummated as God and Man. He will send the Spirit, in virtue of His ascended Manhood, and the perpetual reception of that Manhood into the Godhead.

To sum up. Jesus enquired of the Father, and in answer to the enquiry of the Christ, God gave the Spirit. The Spirit became the Messenger of the Father; and His sphere of work was to be the name of the Son. This Spirit became God's Messenger concerning the Son, vindicating His work and His teaching. By virtue of the perfect union of the Son with the Father, the Spirit is the gift of the Son.

IX

THE CHARACTER OF THE SPIRIT

THE teaching of Christ concerning the character of the Spirit is set forth first in the words: *And I will pray the Father, and He shall give you another Comforter.*[1] This word *Comforter* conveys the first thought concerning the character of the Spirit. It is indeed impossible to find a translation that will reveal everything contained within the great word *Paraclete.* It is conceded that originally the word had what may be spoken of as a passive meaning. It indicated one called to the side of another, and therefore one who, by his coming, annulled the condition of orphanage or desolateness. But then, in its use, both in Classic and New Testament Greek, the word passed into another realm, becoming active, and suggesting the thought of intercession, advocacy, pleading. The word is peculiar to the writings of John. It occurs four times in his Gospel, once in his Epistle. In the Gospel it is translated *Comforter;* in the Epistle, *Advocate.* In the Gospel it

[1] John xiv. 16.

is used of the Spirit; in the Epistle it is used of Christ. The use of it, in the Epistle, is that of Christ standing in the presence of God, as the Advocate of the believer, the Representative, the Intercessor, the Pleader. That is the word and idea used of the Spirit in these discourses of Christ. It is, first, one called to the side of another. That surely was the first thought in the mind of the Lord. He had ever been accessible to these men. They had been able to approach Him with their questionings and perplexities. He was about to leave them, but they were not to be deserted. Another was to take His place, and annul the condition of orphanage. The Spirit is therefore the Spirit of love, banishing the sense of despair and desolateness.

The word *Paraclete* also suggests the thought of an active friendship. He will come, not to plead with God for men—that is the work of Jesus—but to plead with men for God, to intercede with men for Christ, and to win, by His intercession, the whole territory of man's being for the dominance of the living Lord Whom He represents. In this great word there are infinite stretches of meaning. To the waiting people of God the character of the Spirit is love; He will come to fill the gap, to take the place of the tender Christ, to be to the orphaned disciples a Comforter nigh at hand—to comfort them, and to do it by pleading within them the cause of their absent Lord and Master.

Another fact concerning the character of the Spirit is

contained in the words *the Spirit of truth.* He is the inner life of truth, the fact of truth, and therefore will give the exposition of truth. These subjects necessarily overlap each other. This phrase *the Spirit of truth*[1] has its most wonderful explanation in the mission of the Spirit; but it is used here only as revealing His character. How fitting and beautiful this wonderful economy, that the Spirit, Who is Himself the Spirit of truth, should come to be Intercessor for, and Administrator of the affairs of the One Who said, *I am the . . . truth.*[2]

Another fact is declared concerning the character of the Spirit: *the Comforter, even the Holy Spirit.*[3] The Spirit of holiness—this reveals the moral character of the Spirit, and so declares the proper use and ultimate issue of truth.

And yet again: *He shall teach you all things.—He shall bear witness.*[4] He is the Spirit of revelation, the Spirit of illumination.

These sayings of the Master record His teaching concerning the character of the Spirit. He is the Spirit of love, the Comforter; the Spirit of truth, thrice repeated; the Spirit of holiness, the Holy Spirit; the Spirit of revelation, the One Who witnesses and teaches.

[1] John xiv. 17, xv. 26, xvi. 13. [2] John xiv. 6. [3] John xiv. 26. [4] John xiv. 26, xv. 26.

X

THE MISSION OF THE SPIRIT

JESUS also declared in these discourses the nature of the mission of the Spirit. First, His mission to the disciples: *And I will pray the Father, and He shall give you another Comforter, that He may be with you for ever, even the Spirit of truth: Whom the world cannot receive; for it beholdeth Him not, neither knoweth Him: ye know Him; for He abideth with you, and shall be in you.*[1] Here are two great statements.

First, that the mission of the Spirit is to abide with the people of God. The children of God have no need to pray that the Spirit may be given to them: *that He may be with you for ever.* Then the Master proceeds to lay emphasis upon the method in which He will abide: *He abideth with you, and shall be in you.* The Spirit abides with the Church, by taking up His abode in the individual. He is no longer a transient Guest, but the indwelling life of the believer; and He creates and maintains, in spite of all apparent breaking up, the one cath-

[1] John xiv. 16, 17.

olic Church of Christ. His work with regard to the believer is revealed: *He shall teach you all things, and bring to your remembrance all that I said unto you.—He shall bear witness of Me.*[1]*—He shall guide you into all the truth.*[2]*—He shall declare unto you the things that are to come.—He shall glorify Me.*[3]

Secondly, His mission to the world: *And He, when He is come, will convict the world in respect of sin, and of righteousness, and of judgment:*[4] of sin, as having a new centre—*of sin, because they believe not on Me;* of righteousness, as having a new possibility—*I go to the Father;* and of judgment, as being accomplished—*the prince of this world hath been judged.* This is considered more fully in a subsequent chapter.[5]

[1] John xiv. 26. [2] John xv. 26. [3] John xvi. 13, 14. [4] John xvi. 8-11. [5] Chapter xiv.

XI

THE RESULTS OF THE SPIRIT'S COMING

THE teaching of Jesus is clear also as to the results of the Spirit's work: *I will not leave you desolate: I come unto you.*[1] Orphanage is to cease; there is to be no desolateness. This has been dealt with as part of the work of the Spirit. Considered from the side of the experience of the believer, it is indeed full of the deepest comfort. The sense of loneliness never comes to the soul born of the Spirit and living in perpetual obedience to Him. Men hunger after the personal presence of the Christ; but, in proportion as they are yielded to the Holy Spirit, they have that presence, and that in a sense which was impossible to His disciples, while He was here upon earth. He was then limited and localized, and men had to wait for an opportunity of converse. To-day He is ever with every member of the Body; and for fellowship, the elements of time and place with their necessary limitations, are absent.

Again: *But the Comforter, even the Holy Spirit,*

[1] John xiv. 18.

Whom the Father will send in My name, He shall teach you all things, and bring to your remembrance all that I said unto you. Peace I leave with you; My peace I give unto you.[1] The two verses are intimately connected. All the sense of peace that resulted from the presence and comradeship of Christ, becomes perpetual in the new and clearer realization of Himself and His teaching resulting from the abiding of the Spirit. The way in which the Master gave His peace was not as the world giveth, because He gave it by the gift of the Comforter. The second result of the presence of the Spirit is that of peace.

Again: *But when the Comforter is come, Whom I will send unto you from the Father, even the Spirit of truth, which proceedeth from the Father, He shall bear witness of Me: and ye also bear witness, because ye have been with Me from the beginning.*[2] The third result of the Spirit's work is power to witness. This declaration is closely connected with that statement of Peter: *We are witnesses of these things; and so is the Holy Spirit.*[3] The power to witness, according to the prophecy of Christ, and the testimony of Peter, was by the coming of the Spirit.

One other result: *He shall glorify Me: for He shall take of Mine, and shall declare it unto you. All things whatsoever the Father hath are Mine: therefore said I, that He taketh of Mine, and shall declare it unto you.*

[1] John xiv. 26, 27. [2] John xv. 26, 27. [3] Acts v.

A little while, and ye behold Me no more; and again a little while, and ye shall see Me.[1] The Lord did not here refer to His second coming, but to the fact that when the Spirit came He would come by the Spirit, and men would see Him in the ministry of the Spirit. The last result, then, of the Spirit's work is that of vision.

Gather up these four results. Christians are not orphans, and therefore not desolate. Peace is theirs—peace which Christ gives, as the world cannot give, through the ministry of a Person ever present. In the strength of that peace they become His witnesses, because they have a perpetual vision of the Lord.

This is a brief analysis of the Master's teaching concerning the Spirit. The unfolding of all that is contained within this teaching is to be found, historically, in the Acts of the Apostles and the subsequent history of the Church, and, doctrinally, in the Epistles.

The teaching of Jesus is unified truth; and the interpretation of all that follows must ever be in harmony with the principles laid down in these most wonderful discourses. There is much of glory and beauty revealed in the Acts and in the Epistles, which is the blossoming into flower and fruit of that which is here in root and principle.

[1] John xvi. 14-16.

BOOK V

THE PENTECOSTAL AGE

When God of old came down from heaven,
    In power and wrath He came;
Before His feet the clouds were riven,
    Half darkness and half flame.

*   *   *   *   *   *

But when He came the second time,
    He came in power and love;
Softer than gale at morning prime
    Hover'd His holy Dove.

The fires that rush'd on Sinai down
    In sudden torrents dread,
Now gently light, a glorious crown,
    On every sainted head.

Like arrows went those lightnings forth,
    Wing'd with the sinner's doom;
But these, like tongues o'er all the earth,
    Proclaiming life to come.

And as on Israel's awe-struck ear
    The voice, exceeding loud,
The trump, that angels wake to hear,
    Thrill'd from the deep, dark cloud,—

So, when the Spirit of our God
    Came down His flock to find,
A voice from heaven was heard abroad,
    A rushing, mighty wind.

*   *   *   *   *   *

It fills the Church of God; it fills
    The sinful world around;
Only in stubborn hearts and wills
    No place for it is found.

J. Keble.

XII

PENTECOST

THE Master finished His teaching, and passed to His Cross. Having accomplished its sacred work, He rose from the dead, tarried for forty days among His disciples, appearing to them for special purposes, and giving them *commandments through the Holy Spirit.*[1] He then ascended, leaving them one immediate instruction—that they should wait for the advent of the Spirit. He had told them that they were to *go into all the world, and preach the Gospel to the whole creation;*[2] He had told them also that they were to *make disciples of all the nations, baptizing them into the name of the Father and of the Son and of the Holy Spirit.*[3] He had given them instructions conditioning all the service that lay before them; and then He charged them that they were not to begin any of the work until they were endued with power from on high. He left upon them that one restricting word: *He charged them not to depart from Jerusalem, but to wait for the promise of the Father.*[4] No command was given to these men to pray

[1] Acts i. 2. [2] Mark xvi. 15. [3] Matt. xxviii. 19. [4] Acts i. 4.

for the Comforter, nor is it chronicled that they did so. It is somewhat remarkable that commentators almost without exception seem to have taken it for granted that the ten days of waiting were spent in prayer for the Holy Spirit. Neither in the command of Jesus, nor in the chronicled facts, is there any warrant for imagining that such was the case. They were waiting. It is certainly stated that they gave themselves to prayer; but it is not asserted that this was for the Holy Spirit.

During that time they fell into an undoubted blunder, when they endeavored to choose a successor to Judas. Having selected certain men, they proceeded to cast lots to decide which of them should be in the apostolic succession. It is evident that the one upon whom the lot fell never was an apostle in the intention of the Master. The one chosen by the Lord to fill the gap was Saul of Tarsus. When the City of God, described in Revelation, shall be perfect and complete, it is to have twelve foundations, and in the foundations the names of the twelve apostles of the Lamb; and the name of Paul, not Matthias, will surely be the twelfth. Instead of waiting, they proceeded to make appointments. It is no more possible to appoint an officer in the Church, than to preach the Gospel, save by the guidance of the Spirit of God.

After ten days the Holy Spirit was poured out upon the waiting company in that upper room in Jerusalem.

As He came, there was a sound like a mighty rushing wind, heard not only by the people there assembled, but by Jerusalem at large; for it is declared that when the people heard the sound they ran together to see what these things could be. Beside this symbolism that appealed to hearing, the coming was one that appealed to sight; fire, parting asunder, sat in the form of a tongue upon the head of each disciple. Beyond this twofold miracle of sight and sound, there was the wonderful bestowment of the gift of tongues, by which the baptized men and women spoke in other languages than their own.

The place Pentecost occupied in the Divine economy was of great importance.

(i) The Holy Spirit was poured out upon the Day of Pentecost as a gift of God. Man had no claim upon God for that great gift; He was not poured out in answer to any prayer of man, nor on account of any merit in man. He was, as was the gift of Jesus, a gift of grace which all received as from God.

(ii) The pouring out of the Spirit at Pentecost was dependent upon the presence in heaven of Him Who was dead and is alive for evermore. Because of the work that He had wrought, in which satisfaction had been given to righteousness, God poured His Spirit upon man, for the initiation of a new movement and the ushering in of a new dispensation.

(iii) Pentecost was the coming of God the Holy

Spirit to realize His own ideal in human character, by the administration of the work of Jesus, in its redemptive, possessive, and dominant aspects. It was the coming of God as Administrator, in order that the work which He had done as Saviour might become a real fact within the experience and the character of men of whom He should be able to obtain full possession, and in whom, therefore, He should be able to exercise absolute control. By the Holy Spirit, Jesus is henceforth to be Lord, while loyal subjects to His dominion are, by the indwelling of the Spirit, to pass into the realization of the will of God. The coming of the Holy Spirit was the dawn of the brightest day the world had seen since the Fall. It was for the actual impartation to his inner being of the power that should realize the purpose toward which man had been moving through every previous dispensation.

Pentecost affected the whole position of the disciples. In the moment when the Holy Spirit fell upon them, the company of apostles and disciples, about one hundred and twenty in number, were changed from being merely followers of the Messiah into members of the risen Lord. The Lord had exercised a purely Jewish Messiahship; He had fulfilled all the prophecies and promises of the past in His own Person. *He came unto His own*[1] is the word that characterizes His mission up to the Cross; and the Cross is the final emphasis of the other fact—

[1] John i. 11.

that *they that were His own received Him not.* But out of that great nation, which as a nation thus rejected Him, there had been gathered an elect remnant, in succession to that elect remnant which had always existed, even in the ages most characterized by spiritual decadence. Peter, James, John, and others to the number of about five hundred, were followers of Jesus, the Jewish Messiah; and so they continued up to the Day of Pentecost. When one hundred and twenty of these five hundred souls gathered in obedience to the parting command of their Lord, they were still disciples of the Messiah—the little company of people who, amidst the darkness of the nation, had discovered the light of God and had been true to it. They were the people who, failing, trembling in the hour of darkness, had nevertheless loved their Lord through all—the people who had been utterly amazed at the miracle of the Resurrection, and who were now waiting in obedience to the new voice of authority that had sounded in their ears, the voice of their risen Lord. These disciples of the Messiah were waiting for something differing entirely from the expectations of the past; but even now they did not clearly understand their position.

When the Spirit came, they were born again. Hitherto they had been followers of the Christ; and in the purpose of God, in company with faithful Abraham and all who preceded them in a life obedient to the measure of light received, were reckoned as sharers in the work of Christ. But, as an actual fact of life, it was only when the Spirit came—outpoured in baptismal flood, as the result of the work of Jesus upon the Cross—that these men began to live. They were then baptized in the Spirit, and filled with the Spirit.

The result of Pentecost was, moreover, one that affected them not as individuals only, but also in their relation the one to the other. By that baptism they were united into one, and Peter, James, and John were no longer three separate individuals, standing apart from each other while holding the same broad sentiment, but they were members of the one catholic Church. In that moment when the Spirit fell upon the one hundred and twenty or more, the mystical Church of Christ was created. Up to the moment of the coming of the Spirit, they were a concurrence of individuals, a company of units, having a bond of sympathy in their common love to Christ, but no actual, vital, necessary, eternal union. When the Spirit came, the concurrence of individuals was fused into a unity, the Church was formed. The catholic Church was created by the baptism of the Spirit. There was no Church in this sense until the Spirit came; and from then until now the Church has continued. God alone knows the limits of His own Church. It to-day consists of those, in heaven and on earth, who have, by this self-same Spirit, been baptized into the sacred unity of the living Christ. It was when the Spirit fell, that individual disciples of Jesus were transformed from the former association with Him into actual living unity. The mystical Church was formed, by this fusion into a unity, of those who were baptized by the Spirit on the Day of Pentecost.

As the result of the great work of the Son of God, in life, death, resurrection, and ascension, there was poured upon a little company of men and women, who had chosen to suffer with Him, the great gift of the Holy Spirit. They were thus created a corporate unity, one with Christ and with each other, and there was brought into the world a new creation, the Church, consisting of Christ and all those thus united to Him.[1]

The coming of the Spirit and the fusing of these individuals into one great whole affected the relation of the whole race to God. It was the coming into the world of a new temple—the Church. *Ye are a temple of God*[2]—an individual truth, but a collective truth also. It was the coming into the world of that of which the old Temple, with its priesthood, its offerings, and its ritual, was prophetic; it was the building in the world of a dwelling-place of God through the Spirit.

[1] A question arises as to what became of the rest of the five hundred disciples of Jesus who saw Him after His resurrection —*He appeared to above five hundred brethren at once* (1 Cor. xv. 6)—but who did not tarry in obedience to His command in Jerusalem. No definite statement can be made concerning them. It is certain, however, that they were not on the Day of Pentecost included in the Church, their disobedience preventing this. It is probable that, as the time passed on, many of them would become more fully instructed, and by submission would receive the gift. Nothing can be said with any certainty, as nothing has been revealed in Scripture. [2] 1 Cor. iii. 16.

The Temple was the place of praise, whence the song, the chant, and the hallelujah ascended perpetually into the presence of God. Man is created for the glory of God, and *whoso offereth the sacrifice of thanksgiving glorifieth Me.*[1] It is the Divine intention that man should say, not only with his lip, but in every power of his nature, *Hallelujah!* First the Tabernacle, then the Temple, was given to man as a place of praise.

But the Temple meant more than praise; it meant a possibility of prayer. *Is it not written, My house shall be called a house of prayer for all the nations?*[2] It was a point to which humanity might come and tell its agony in the listening ear of Heaven, a place where men might pray. Men are, first, to praise; but praise must ofttimes cease, choked by the sob of sorrow; then let men pray.

Beyond that, the Temple was the place of prophetic utterance—prophecy being, in its largest meaning, a Divine answer to prayer. Prayer is the voice of man in his need speaking to God: prophecy is the voice of God in His power speaking to man. These things had been symbolized in the Temple.

Now those men and women in the upper room—being no longer simply a company, but Christ's Church—form a Divine institution of praise. Through them there is to ascend from the earth to heaven the praise of men. The outsiders will join the praise as they enter the

[1] Ps. l. 23. [2] Mark xi. 17.

Church; they will find the opportunity of praise as they come into the new Temple of God given to man.

That company of people, having now become one Church, is also a medium of prayer. They are a kingdom of priests: that is, a company of individuals who will unite prayer to prayer and intercession to intercession; a company of men and women who will carry on their hearts the surging sorrow of the earth, and will pour its tale out in the listening ear of Heaven; a company of men and women who will always be conscious of the suffering of humanity, and will tell it out to God. The multitudes outside will begin to pray as they enter the Church. Their prayer will become prevailing as they join the new medium of prayer, which is the new Temple, the Church of Jesus Christ.

The Church will not only praise and pray,—all its members have become prophets. They will pass from the upper room, and scatter themselves over the whole earth, reaching out into all the places where men abide. They will not be divided; they will still be the Church. The sigh of Moses long ago, *Would God that all the Lord's people were prophets!*[1] finds its answer in the Pentecostal effusion and the bestowment of the prophetic gift upon the living members of the new Church. Before one hundred years had passed, every known nation and all human institutions had felt the touch of the new power by the prophesying of the Church.

[1] Num. xi. 29.

A new Temple was given to men upon the Day of Pentecost—that is, a new centre of praise, a new power of prayer, and a new power of prophecy. No longer is *Jerusalem the place where men ought to worship;*[1] no longer is *this mountain*, as Christ characterized the Samaritan centre, the only place; but everywhere men may worship God. Christ is the Door of the Church; and men through belief in Him pass thereinto, the Spirit baptizing them into living union with Him. The Temple grows and expands by this incorporation of individual members. Whether in a far-off land or at home, whether in Jerusalem or at the end of the earth, men pass into the new Temple by this self-same Spirit Who was poured out upon the day of Pentecost for their admission into the relationship with God which should fit them for praise, prayer, and prophecy. When Peter handled the keys of the kingdom for the first time, he opened the door to the Jew, and three thousand entered. Then he opened the door to the Gentiles in the house of Cornelius, and the Gentiles began to crowd in. That handling of the keys was not Peter's peculiar prerogative. It was also the prerogative of every member of the Church. It is the prerogative of every person who, as a prophet of the Cross, in the demonstration of the Spirit, speaks to some soul, so that there opens before that soul a vision of the things of the kingdom. That is the true exercise of the power of the keys.[2] Pentecost meant for

[1] John iv. 20. [2] This throws light upon the sacerdotal question. With a strange confusion men have imagined that the keys were

the world the creation of a new Temple, no longer limited, localized, and material, but unlimited, to be found everywhere, and spiritual, for the Spirit is everywhere. Entrance to this Temple is found wherever man in his need and agony submits himself to Christ.

Before closing this chapter, it is necessary to notice the difference between the events of the Day of Pentecost with the period immediately following, and the occurrence in the house of Cornelius with the subsequent history of the Book of the Acts. The whole of the men and women upon whom the Spirit fell on the Day of Pentecost were Jewish; and the period immediately following Pentecost may be spoken of as peculiarly Jewish. There are two remarkable characteristics of the work of the Spirit during that period that ceased immediately afterwards. This period is dealt with in the first nine chapters, and during it there seems to have been an interval between the acceptation of the good tidings concerning the kingdom of God and the reception of the Holy Spirit. People believed the tidings, and yet they did not receive the Holy Spirit. Moreover, there was some intervention on the part of another disciple before the gift of the Spirit was received.[1]

The Gospel was preached to the Gentiles in the house of Cornelius,[2] and it is never again recorded that those who believed in Jesus received the Holy Spirit as a sub-

the symbols of priestly power. They were not. They were the insignia of the prophetic office.

[1] The work of Philip in Samaria and the conversion of Saul are instances. They will be considered in Chapter XV. [2] Acts x.

sequent blessing. The apostles preached the kingdom of God; and when a Jew heard about the kingdom, he did exactly what had been done in the days of Christ's ministry—he thought of earthly power, had no conception of the spiritual reality, and believed in Jesus as a Restorer of the temporal kingdom. His conception was material; and in every such case it was necessary for some more enlightened disciple to teach him the spiritual reality, in order that he might receive the Holy Spirit.

When Peter preached in the house of Cornelius, he announced good tidings of peace, and the lordship of Jesus, and remission of sins. This the Gentiles heard, not from the Jewish standpoint. The story of the kingdom was not all. They heard also the story of salvation from sin. When they believed, it was the whole Gospel, and the Spirit fell upon them straightway. There was no *second blessing*. This, then, represents the normal condition of things under the present dispensation. Men believe in Jesus as King and Saviour, and are baptized by the Spirit into relationship with Him, that being the hour of their new birth, and that in which they become members of the catholic Church of Jesus Christ.

Pentecost, in the economy of God, was the occasion of the outpouring of the Spirit, in answer to the completed work of the Christ, in order that the purpose of God might be realized in the character of men.

Pentecost, in the case of the disciple, was the change

from being merely a follower, a learner, into that of living union with the living Christ

Pentecost, in the case of the world, was the advent in the world of a new Temple consisting of living men, women, and children indwelt by the Spirit of God, for purposes of praise, and prayer, and prophecy.

XIII

THE SPIRIT IN THE CHURCH

ON the Day of Pentecost the coming of the Spirit upon a company of waiting disciples changed them from an aggregation of units into one corporate whole, the Church of the living God. From that moment all the essentials of the Church have been maintained by His abiding therein.

By the creation of the Church a new Temple was given to the world, a new institute for praise, for prayer, and for prophecy. All these functions are fulfilled by the abiding of the Spirit in the Church. The incense of praise is offered by the inspiration of the Spirit; the intercession of prayer is maintained by the whole company of those who pray in the Holy Spirit; the work of prophecy, in its fullest meaning of forth-telling, is carried forward by such as are witnesses, in co-operation with the Holy Spirit, to the eternal verities of God.

The Letters to the Corinthians deal with New Testament Church orders; and in the first, the apostle having discussed certain disorders that had arisen in the church at Corinth, proceeded to deal with ecclesiastical matters; and, in conclusion, he revealed a threefold fact concerning the relation of the Spirit to the whole Church of God. *Now concerning spiritual gifts, brethren.*[1] Both in the Authorized and in the Revised Versions the word *gifts* is in italics. The term πνευματικά[2] covers a subject far wider than that of the gifts of the Spirit. It is undoubtedly with the gifts that the apostle specially dealt; but he opened his subject by writing: *Brethren, I would not have you ignorant concerning the matters that pertain to the Spirit.* Then he made three main statements concerning these matters. First, he declared the Holy Spirit to be the Defender of the Church's faith: *No man can say, Jesus is Lord, but in the Holy Spirit.*[3] In the second place, he declared the Holy Spirit to be the Inspiration of the Church's service: *There are diversities of gifts, but the same Spirit. . . . But all these worketh the one and the same Spirit, dividing to each one severally even as He will.*[4] And, thirdly, he declared the Holy Spirit to be the bond of the Church's unity: *For in one Spirit were we all baptized into one body.*[5]

The Holy Spirit is the Defender of the Faith. *No man can say, Jesus is Lord, but in the Holy Spirit.*[6] The old desire for authority in matters of faith and of doctrine is still felt, and is perfectly natural and right. It

[1] I Cor. xii. I. [2] πνευματικῶν, Things of the Spirit, I Cor. xii. I. [3] I Cor. xii. 3. [4] I Cor. xii. 4, 11. [5] I Cor. xii. 13. [6] I Cor. xii. 3.

has ever been realized in the history of the Church. It may safely be said that all great crises in Church history have been the result of a division of opinion as to where the seat of authority really lies in matters of discipline and of doctrine.

The Reformation under Luther was a restoration of the lost doctrine of Justification by Faith; but that, in a further analysis, is a statement of the seat of authority in the matter of forgiveness and of pardon. In that wonderful work which Luther was raised up of God to do, he called men back from seeking authoritative absolution from a man, to seek it from God.

The Oxford movement, the outworking of which in the sacerdotal revival to-day is so manifest, is a startling illustration of this fact. Newman—sweet, strong, sainted soul, from whom those who believe in the alone and undelegated authority of the Spirit radically differ in many particulars, but with whom all saints have communion still in his love for the Master—entered the Roman church because he sought for authority, and his intellect found a species of rest in what he believed to be the authority of that church.

Protestants are perpetually being told that they have no centre of authority. This statement is due to the fact that those who make it forget that the one, the abiding, and the only centre of authority, in matters of faith and doctrine, is the Holy Spirit. That is the teaching of this declaration, passed over too often as though it were simply a statement of initial matters. That it certainly is; but it is infinitely more. That Jesus is Lord is the centre of all Christian doctrine; everything else grows out of it. *No man can say, Jesus is Lord, but in the Holy Spirit.*[1] All true systems of theology are but the subdivision and application to varied and varying circumstances of this central fact, that Jesus is Lord.

The same apostle stated: *For to this end Christ died, and lived again, that He might be Lord of both the dead and the living.*[2] The Lordship of Christ is the doctrinal fact which is the centre of all others; the Lordship of Christ is the practical fact which is the issue of the doctrine. Doctrine and duty are wedded in the scheme of Christianity. Every doctrine has its expression in some duty; all creed has its out-blossoming in character.

The inner historic fact of Christianity is Christ, living, dying, rising, reigning; and the purpose of His living, dying, rising, and reigning is that He should be Lord both of the dead and of the living. The relation which the ministry of the Holy Spirit bears to that doctrine is of the closest. *No man can say, Jesus is Lord, but in the Holy Spirit.* It is the Holy Spirit Who first reveals Christ to the heart of man, so that man says, in response to the revelation: *Thou art my Lord.* It is the work of the Spirit to take this inner, central part of Christian doctrine, and make it real to men, so that they respond

[1] 1 Cor. xii. 3. [2] Rom. xiv. 9.

to the doctrine by fulfilling the duty. That initial work having been done, it is the Spirit Who unfolds the revelation step by step,—*precept upon precept; . . . —line upon line; here a little, there a little,*[1]—by so much as men are able to bear it, giving new vision of the beauty and glory of the Master, for life and character. Every vision of Christ granted to the believer has been the result of the presence in that believer of the Holy Spirit, Who alone gives grace to say in new realms of life, in new vistas of outlook, that Jesus is Lord.

Thus, whether the look is backward upon the past of sin, He is Lord, and has *blotted out the bond written in ordinances that was against us;*[2] or whether it is at the present condition of our hearts, He is Lord, and will have dominion over the nature until the Divine purpose be realized; or whether it is forward to the end of life, He is still Lord, and fills the horizon, so that souls, homed in His kingdom, wait for His coming; or whether it is round upon the world, He even there is Lord, and

Through the ages one increasing purpose runs,
And the thoughts of men are widen'd with the process of the suns,—

widened—slowly but surely, nevertheless—to a conception of the Lordship of the Son of God.

The Holy Spirit is the one and only Defender of this Faith; and every fight for orthodoxy other than that which is aimed at bringing men to fulness of spiritual

[1] Isa. xxviii. 10. [2] Col. ii. 14.

life is futile. Life in the Holy Spirit is the safeguard of purity of doctrine.

In order to emphasize this fact, consider three great landmarks in the history of the Church—the Reformation, the Evangelical revival, and the spiritual movements of to-day.

The declension that led to the Reformation, and the Reformation itself, are proofs of the fact that purity of doctrine is only maintained by the Holy Spirit. The Reformation was necessary that the truth of Justification by faith should be restated, because the Church had wandered from spiritual to material conceptions, and the Holy Spirit had been slighted and contemned. To borrow the figure of the old Hebrew prophet, men had gone to Egypt for horses upon which to fight God's battles; they had asked and obtained the patronage of the State in matters religious. Constantine had become the patron of Christianity; the Holy Spirit had been dethroned from His proper position. The result was the materializing of religious thought and character, until men had lost the doctrine of Justification by Faith, because they had lost their loyalty to the Holy Spirit. The doctrine was restored through a man to whom the Spirit gave a new vision of the lost truth. Luther declared the doctrine in the face of the world; the Spirit spoke through him; the eyes of men were opened, and there was a return to the Christian doctrine, because there was a return to the Holy Spirit.

The Evangelical revival illustrates the same thing. This was made necessary by the fact that the Church of God had lost its vision of the truth of Sanctification. John Wesley said that he had been raised up in order that he might promote Holiness throughout the land; and he declared at the beginning of that movement that if he could find one hundred men who feared nothing but sin he would move the world. God gave him his hundred men, and he did move the world. He revolutionized the thought of this country, so that to-day the spiritual results of the Methodist movement are not measured by the number of its adherents, but by the ever-increasing understanding of the doctrine of Holiness in all the Churches. John Wesley did not discover some new doctrine, save as a man may discover that which has been hidden; it was the old apostolic truth that he brought to light. It had been lost, because the Holy Spirit had neither been acknowledged as a Person nor recognized as the Centre of authority in Church life. This land had passed under the deadly blight of material conceptions of Christianity. The fox-hunting parson, who cared neither for God, man, nor devil, but only for tithes and hounds, was the representative of Christianity who cursed the times. He was dismissed by the return of men through John Wesley and his holy club at Oxford to the truth of the sanctification of the believer through the submission of human lives to the government of the Spirit. To borrow Dr. Steele's phrase, *the*

Conservator of orthodoxy in every successive age is the Holy Spirit.[1]

Creeds do not ensure orthodoxy, for no individual church holds all the truth of the Church. The great body of truth is the property of the catholic Church, not of any section, nor yet of any individual member thereof. Sometimes one is asked if he *hold the truth.* Certainly not, for no single person can hold the truth. He may see one side of it—and that one side is almost more than he can bear—while another person sees another side. One is not to be angry with the other because neither sees all the facets of the lustrous gem, nor is the other to decline to work with the one because both do not alike include in their understanding all the angles thereof. To this man is given a vision of the individual application of the work of Christ; to another, the vision of its social application; to yet another, that of the national and international application. And the man who sees the individual aspect of that work has no right to anathematize the man who only sees the national aspect. One man feels that there is laid upon his heart the great message of a Christian doctrine and a living Christ to the nations; and he so feels the impulse of that upon him, that he must give up his work with individuals, and appeal, as much as one voice may, to the nation, from the floor of some legislative chamber. It cannot be said that such a man is not doing God's work.

[1]Daniel Steele, D.D., author of *Milestone Papers*, etc.

A man is not necessarily fulfilling the final and only work of the ministry when he is in the pulpit. Stepping from the pulpit and from the work of dealing with individual men about conversion and spiritual upbuilding would be to some a degradation of life. But if another man has another outlook, and would speak to masses of men, and to nations of the earth, about the way in which Christ would have society conducted and nations order their government, the preacher in his pulpit has no right to despise that man. Nay, to one is given one vision of Christ, and to another yet another; but no man holds all the truth, as no man has all the gifts.

In the catholic Church, by the Spirit, is contained the whole truth; and in the catholic Church, by the Spirit, is contained all the gifts necessary for the declaration thereof. The catholic Church, inspired by the Spirit, indwelt by the Spirit, is a divine institution infinitely larger than human sight can compass, human statistics declare, or human understanding perfectly comprehend.

Life in the Spirit is necessarily, therefore, the inspiration of, and the equipment for service. Attempts may be made to organize and apportion to every man his work, giving to one the individual, to another the social, and to a third the national work; and subdividing these things, it may be planned that this man shall preach the gospel of forgiveness, that man the gospel of holiness, and another the gospel of the coming Christ. For the orderly execution of these matters there may be distinctions, and degrees, and seasons, and symbols. The Spirit of God cannot, however, be crowded into small human channels and ideas. What absolute folly is evidenced by all such attempts! The catholic Church is not bounded by loose ropes of sand, it is not maintained in order by small definitions, but by the Spirit, Who is the Conservator of its orthodoxy and the Inspiration of its service. He gives His gifts severally as He will; and not along such restricted lines of communication as the laying on of hands, but through the broad river of His indwelling of the Church, come the gifts as well as the graces of God.

If the Spirit be the Defender of the Church's faith and the Inspiration of the Church's service, He is also the Bond of the Church's unity. *In one Spirit were we all baptized into one body.*[1] The Door of the Church is Jesus Christ; and reverently the figure may be carried further—the Holy Spirit guards the Door. From that Pentecostal effusion to this hour, the Holy Spirit has guarded the entrance to the Church of Christ, and admitted all its members by His own baptism. Men and women have ever passed into the catholic Church by the one Door, and entrance has ever been by the baptism of the Holy Spirit, apart from which it is impossible for any soul to come into living union with Christ, the Head of the Church. Consequently, the whole company of those who are in the Church are energized and impulsed by the same Spirit. There is one body and

[1] 1 Cor. xii. 13.

one Spirit—one body, as the human body is one having different members, each with its own function, but only one life. The hand has not a separate existence from the foot, but each has the one life; so, in the catholic Church, there are many members having varying functions, but all are impulsed by the one life.

The Holy Spirit is the life of the catholic Church, and in that life lies the great bond of its union. The Church is one and undivided. To all outward seeming it is divided, and each division arrogates to itself the name of the Church, until at last one most carefully separated division declares that all the rest are systems and sects, and it alone gives outward revelation of what the true Church is.

The fact is that men do not know the bounds of the catholic Church, which is smaller than the records of the churches show, and is yet greater than them all. There are living members of that Church in all the churches, and it may be that on the rolls of the churches are names which are not on the roll of the catholic Church. Those are members thereof who are baptized into union with Christ by the Holy Spirit. The Lord knows them; and being members of His one Church, they can sing the words of Baring-Gould's hymn in a far higher sense than some people imagine:—

We are not divided;
All one body we,
One in hope and doctrine,
One in charity.

It may be objected that the Church is not one in doctrine. The catholic Church is one in doctrine, and this is its central word: Jesus is Lord. Whether men express that truth to swing of censer and swell of music, or to the beat of the drum and the blare of the trumpet, or without any of these accompaniments, matters far less than is imagined.

The life of the Church came, not by the will of man, nor by a ceremony of human invention, but by the baptism of the Spirit; and the great unity of that Church is still maintained by the indwelling of all its members by the Holy Spirit. The true consciousness of this unity of the Spirit, is the love concerning which Paul wrote, and which finds its manifestation toward the unit and the aggregate of units which make up the whole. The unity of the Church can only be realized in full spiritual life. Acts of Uniformity cannot make the Church one: that is the original and continuous work of the Spirit. Of that one great Church of Christ some of its members are at home with the Lord, some are passing through the earth, and some are coming up out of to-morrow; and the Spirit is the Keeper of the unity, which cannot be broken. Presently out of all the seeming disagreement and disruption will come the glorious Church of the First-born, without spot or wrinkle or any such thing.

XIV

THE SPIRIT IN THE WORLD

THE ministry of the Spirit in the present age is by no means confined within the limits of the Church. Scripture very clearly reveals the intention as being far wider; and the history of the centuries proves the accomplishment to be in keeping with the intention.

There are three portions of Scripture which may be examined as throwing light on this subject. First, a prophetic utterance, the fulfilment of which Peter claimed as being accomplished on the Day of Pentecost; secondly, the express declaration of the Lord concerning the Spirit's ministry in the world; and, lastly, the teaching of Paul and John concerning the work of the Holy Spirit as opposed to the work of the spirit of evil. All these deal with a present ministry of the Spirit which in some sense is united to the work of the Church, but is also apart from and beyond it.

First, the prophecy: *These are not drunken, as ye suppose; seeing it is but the third hour of the day; but this is that which hath been spoken by the prophet Joel;*[1]

[1] Acts ii. 15-18.

And it shall be in the last days, saith God,
I will pour forth of My Spirit upon all flesh:
And your sons and your daughters shall prophesy,
And your young men shall see visions,
And your old men shall dream dreams:
Yea and on My servants and on My handmaidens in those days
Will I pour forth of My Spirit; and they shall prophesy.

The term *all flesh* is an expression which is uniformly used in the Old Testament Scriptures with reference to the whole race. The exceptions are to be found repeatedly in the Pentateuch and once in the Book of Daniel,[1] where the expression *all flesh* refers not only to the human race but to everything having life. The sense of the phrase cannot be narrowed to anything smaller than the whole human family; and the statement here is clear and distinct—the utterance of the prophet long years before Pentecost, and the utterance of the apostle on the Day of Pentecost, claiming the fulfilment of the old prophecy, that the Spirit should be poured upon *all flesh.*

The link between the prophecy and its fulfilment is revealed in the Gospel of John: *In the beginning was the Word, and the Word was with God, and the Word was God. . . . And the Word became flesh, and dwelt among us.*[2] The eternal Word took upon Him a nature

[1] Dan. iv. 12. [2] John i. 1, 14.

common to the race, and therein wrought righteousness and accomplished redemption. Consequently, when He ascended on high to receive gifts for men, He received the Spirit, and by His outpouring upon disciples, the Church was formed. The Pentecostal effusion had, however, another and far wider significance. The Spirit was poured upon all flesh, so that the whole human race was thereby brought into a new relationship with Him as the result of the work of Jesus Christ. Just as the Word took the common flesh of humanity, and associated Himself with the whole race; so, as the result of the work He did while thus associated, the Spirit was poured not merely upon the company of disciples, but also upon *all flesh*. This is the larger outlook upon the mission of the Spirit. Let there be no minimizing of the value of this great statement.

There is, however, a distinct difference between the relationship that the Spirit bears to the believer and to the unbeliever. The Spirit is in the believer, and he by that indwelling is kept in union with Christ. The Spirit strives with the unbeliever as a Spirit of conviction, of reasoning, wooing him in patience to the way of God. The difference is most marked, yet the ministry of the Spirit is a ministry which touches all men.

Secondly, the declaration of Christ in the Paschal discourses: *And He, when He is come, will convict the world in respect of sin, and of righteousness, and of judgment: of sin, because they believe not on Me; of righteousness, because I go to the Father, and ye behold Me no more; of judgment, because the prince of this world hath been judged.*[1] This is the first aspect of the ministry of the Spirit among men. He came not merely to reveal the things of Christ to the Church, but to *convict the world of sin, of righteousness, and of judgment.* In the Authorized Version the word *convict* is rendered *reprove.* It is a word the inner thought of which is not revealed by the translation *convict.* Bishop Westcott, in his luminous exposition of the Gospel of John, says that this word has in it four shades of meaning: first, an authoritative examination of the facts; secondly, unquestionable proof; thirdly, decisive judgment; and, lastly, punitive power.

The mission of the Holy Spirit with men is that of revealing to them the truth on these subjects, in such a way that they shall be convinced that it is the truth. Concerning sin, men seek to excuse themselves, try to evade the facts; but when the Spirit deals with a man about sin, he cannot escape; and under His illumination man has the same clear vision of righteousness and judgment.

Passing from the word itself to the subject, *He . . . will convict the world in respect of sin, and of righteousness, and of judgment,*[2] it is clear that these three words cover the past, the present, and the future of the outlook of man as a sinner—the history of past sin, the

[1] John xvi. 8-11. [2] John xvi. 8.

present demand for righteousness, and the fear of future judgment. The Spirit takes these three cardinal facts, and places them in their true light, so that men may make no mistake concerning them. The Master declared the testimony the Spirit would bear on these subjects. . . . *Of sin, because they believe not on Me; of righteousness, because I go to the Father, and ye behold Me no more; of judgment, because the prince of this world hath been judged.*[1] That is the threefold revelation which the Spirit is giving to the world to-day, and it demands a closer examination.

Three persons are spoken of: Man, Christ, and Satan —Man in the realm of sin, Christ in the realm of righteousness, Satan in the realm of judgment. Observe next the inter-relation of these three: Man in his relationship to himself, to Christ, and to Satan; Christ in His relationship to Himself, to man, and to Satan; Satan in his relationship to himself, to man, and to Christ.

First, Man in his relationship to the three. Man's relationship to himself is that of a sinner having lost his life, whose sin ceases and is put away when he believes in Jesus. Man's relationship to Christ is that of a sinner for whom He has procured salvation, and through Whose triumph of righteousness man may himself do righteously. Man's relationship to Satan is that of a slave under the prince of this world, but from

[1] John xvi. 9-11.

whose power he is set free, for this prince has been defeated.

Secondly, Christ in His relationship to the three. Christ's relationship to Himself is that of righteousness, for He declared His personal triumph when He said: *I go to the Father.*[1] His relationship to man is that of a Saviour, and therefore man's sin consists in refusal to believe on Him. Christ's relationship to Satan is that of Conqueror, for *the prince of this world hath been judged.*[2]

Lastly, Satan in his relation to the three. Satan, concerning himself, is conquered—*hath been judged*—and is powerless; concerning man, is conquered—*hath been judged*—and therefore can no longer claim man's service; concerning Christ, is conquered—*hath been judged*—and therefore even he must own Him King. There is no other outlook for evil than that of conquest.

Once again: *He, when He is come, will convict the world in respect of sin . . . because they believe not on Me.*[3] With the coming of the Spirit upon all flesh, sin had a new centre. Henceforth sin consists in the refusal to accept the Divine provision of healing and power. No longer is the root-sin that of impurity, or drunkenness, or lust, or pride, or even law-breaking; the root-sin is the refusal to believe on Jesus. If men will believe on Him, in that relationship to Christ which springs from belief, is to be found healing for wounds, and

[1] John xvi. 17. [2] John xvi. 11. [3] John xvi. 8, 9.

strength which issues in victory. The Spirit declares that the sin lies, not in the fact of passion, but in the refusal to let the Master master the passion.

The Spirit has also come to reveal the truth about righteousness. If the revelation of sin be that of a new centre, the revelation of righteousness is, consequently, that of a new possibility. *Of righteousness, because I go to the Father.*[1] In the height of that glory, which mortal eyes may by no means look upon, is God's perfect Man, the One Who said, *I go to the Father.* Not simply by virtue of His own righteousness did He go, but bearing into the presence of the Father the marks of that death on the Cross, by which He liberated His life, that it might become the force of renewal for man. The Spirit comes to bring to men the gospel of a new possibility of righteousness.

Lastly, the Spirit's revelation of judgment is concerned with a new exercise thereof. A common mistake, in quoting this passage, is that of adding the words *to come* after *judgment.* The confusion of thought which this reveals is obvious; for the judgment here referred to is not that which is to come, but that which is already accomplished. The Judgment Day is not to be one of twenty-four hours, but of long duration, an age in itself, of which the closing event will be the final assize before the Great White Throne. That stupendous transaction will simply be the unfolding of the facts

[1] John xvi. 10.

which are present to-day, because the prince of this world hath been judged. Righteousness has had its conflict with evil, and has won in the fight. The head of the enemy of the race has been bruised, even though the heel of the Victor was wounded in the process. *The prince of this world hath been judged;* and the things that must pass and perish are evil things and unrighteous things, while the things that cannot be shaken and that will remain are righteous things, pure things, and beautiful things, yea, all the things of God. Judgment is fixed, doom is marked, destiny is sealed, by the Cross of Jesus Christ. If men fling in their lot with things which are doomed and judged, then they must share the doom and judgment which have been passed upon them by the Cross of Calvary; but if they turn their backs upon doomed things, and lift their eyes toward the things that abide, the heavenly things where Christ is, the upper things, the conquering things, then for them judgment was borne upon the Cross, and they have entered into justification-life. Thus the ministry of the Spirit in the world to-day is that of revealing the truth concerning sin, righteousness, and judgment.

Thirdly, the teaching of Paul and John is clear that the Spirit has yet another ministry in the world to-day—that, namely, of hindering the full manifestation of sin. Paul and John in their Epistles give testimony to the fact that the Holy Spirit is the ever-present Force denying, hindering, thwarting, the outworking of evil.

This is clearly revealed by comparison of certain of their writings.

. . . *The man of sin . . . the son of perdition, he that opposeth and exalteth himself against all that is called God or that is worshipped; so that he sitteth in the temple of God, setting himself forth as God.*[1] That is a description of antichrist as he will be. *The mystery of lawlessness doth already work. . . . And then shall be revealed the lawless one.*[2] The apostle thus states that there is a mystery of iniquity, a *mystery of lawlessness*, at work among men, and that there is a day coming when that mystery will have a manifestation in an actual person, *the lawless one will be revealed.*

John, writing on this same theme, says: *Who is the liar but he that denieth that Jesus is the Christ? This is the antichrist, even he that denieth the Father and the Son.*[3]—*Every spirit which confesseth not Jesus is not of God: and this is the spirit of the antichrist, whereof ye have heard that it cometh; and now it is in the world already.*[4] This is practically the same teaching—namely, that there is a spirit of antichrist, a spirit of *the mystery of lawlessness*, in the world, and that at some period in the future it is to have a manifestation in a person. It is the spirit which denies God, not necessarily with the blatant blasphemy of public speech, but it may be with all cultured correctness of life. It is that which denies God, that which denies Christ.

[1] 2 Thess. ii. 3, 4. [2] 2 Thess. ii. 7, 8. [3] 1 John ii. 22. [4] John iv. 3.

Paul distinctly states that there is another force which holds this force of evil in check: *And now ye know that which restraineth. . . . The mystery of lawlessness doth already work: only there is One that restraineth now, until He be taken out of the way.*[1] This is a plain declaration that the spirit of evil is at work, and also that there is a Force which restrains. He does not say it is the Holy Spirit. There has been a great deal of controversy about this particular passage, and attempts have been made to show that it had regard to the Roman power in the past. John, however, makes it clear Who the One that restraineth is: *Hereby know ye the spirit of God: every spirit which confesseth that Jesus Christ is come in the flesh is of God: and every spirit which confesseth not Jesus is not of God: and this is the spirit of the antichrist.*[2] Here the two things are placed in opposition,—the spirit of antichrist, which denies Jesus Christ and denies God; the Spirit of God, Who announces the Christ of God, and teaches men how to call Him Lord.

These two forces are still at work in the world,—the spirit of evil, the leaven that is undoing men everywhere; and the Spirit of God, Who restrains and holds in check the force of evil.

All the great forces which are antagonistic to God have been thus hindered, restrained, checked, flung back upon themselves during the last nineteen hundred years.

[1] 2 Thess. ii. 6, 7. [2] 1 John iv. 2, 3.

The ministry of the Spirit is larger than His ministry in the Church; it is world-wide, and is always based upon the work of the Christ. Whether to the Church or to the world, the Spirit has no message but the message of Jesus Christ. To the man in the Church, and to the whole Church, He is revealing the Christ in new beauty and new glory. To the world He is revealing sin, righteousness, and judgment in their relation to the Christ. The Spirit is poured upon all flesh; and, in co-operation with the Church, He convinces of sin, and of righteousness, and of judgment. Therein lie the heart, the centre, and the responsibility of foreign missionary work. *How shall they hear without a preacher? and how shall they preach, except they be sent?*[1] The Holy Spirit is waiting in the far-distant places of the earth for the voice of anointed man to preach, in order that through that instrumentality He may carry on His work of convicting of sin, and of righteousness, and of judgment.

Beyond that, there is this other marvellous ministry which is too often lost sight of. By His presence in the world He is restraining the out-working of iniquity, and is checking, hindering, and driving back every attempted combination of the forces of evil for the swamping of the Church, and the hindering of the kingdom. The Spirit's restraining work will go forward until the moment has come when the number of the elect is complete.

[1] Rom. x. 14, 15.

Then shall the Spirit be withdrawn when the Church is called away, in order that iniquity may be manifested and smitten to its final doom, and the glorious kingdom of our God be set up.[1]

[1] The only sense in which the Spirit is withdrawn is that which characterizes His special work in this age—that, namely, of conserving the Church and preventing the progress of evil to finality. He will carry on His work of striving with men as He did prior to the Deluge, but with results more glorious. This, however, is another subject and a part of prophetic study.

BOOK VI

THE SPIRIT IN THE INDIVIDUAL

Thou Breath from still eternity,
  Breathe o'er my spirit's barren land—
The pine-tree and the myrtle-tree
  Shall spring amidst the desert sand,
And where Thy living water flows
The waste shall blossom as the rose.

May I in will and deed and word
  Obey Thee as a little child;
And keep me in Thy love, my Lord,
  For ever holy, undefiled;
Within me teach and strive and pray,
Lest I should choose my own wild way.

O Spirit, Stream that by the Son
  Is open'd to us crystal pure,
Forth-flowing from the heavenly Throne
  To waiting hearts and spirits poor,
Athirst and weary do I sink
Beside Thy waters, there to drink.

My spirit turns to Thee and clings,
  All else forsaking, unto Thee,
Forgetting all created things,
  Remembering only *God in me.*
O living Stream, O gracious Rain,
None wait for Thee, and wait in vain.

G. Tersteegen.

XV

THE BAPTISM OF THE SPIRIT

IN dealing with these matters of the Spirit, it is wise to keep, as far as possible, to the terms of the New Testament; and it would be an enormous gain if they were used only as they are used in Scripture. The term *the baptism of the Spirit* has been very generally misunderstood, and therefore misapplied. It has been used as though it were synonymous with *the filling of the Spirit;* and, consequently, some persons speak of the baptism of the Spirit as *a second blessing.* They teach that it is necessary to ask for, and to wait for, and to expect this baptism of the Spirit, as something different from and beyond conversion. That is a view utterly unauthorized by Scripture. The baptism of the Spirit is the primary blessing; it is, in short, the blessing of regeneration. When a man is baptized with the Spirit, he is born again. There is, however, an essential difference between that initial blessing and the blessing into which thousands of God's people have been entering during recent years—the difference between the baptism of the Spirit and the filling of the Spirit.

In the majority of cases in the experience of believers, the filling of the Spirit is realized after the baptism. They are identical in the purpose of God, but there is a difference in the experience. So important is it that Christian people should have a clear understanding of what the baptism of the Spirit really is, that it will be well to review the whole of the passages in the New Testament in which the words are used, in order to a correct appreciation of the true significance of the phrase.

John . . . when he saw many of the Pharisees and Sadducees coming to his baptism, said unto them . . . I indeed baptize you with water unto repentance: but He that cometh after me is mightier than I, Whose shoes I am not worthy to bear: He shall baptize you with the Holy Spirit and with fire.[1]

John . . . preached, saying . . . I baptized you with water; but He shall baptize you with the Holy Spirit.[2]

John answered, saying unto them all, I indeed baptize you with water; but there cometh He that is mightier than I, the latchet of Whose shoes I am not worthy to unloose: He shall baptize you with the Holy Spirit and with fire.[3]

John answered them, saying. I baptize with water: in the midst of you standeth One Whom ye know not, even He that cometh after me, the latchet of Whose shoe I am

[1] Matt. iii. 4-11. [2] Mark i. 6-8. [3] Luke iii. 16

not worthy to unloose.[1] . . . *And John bare witness, saying, I have beheld the Spirit descending as a dove out of heaven; and it abode upon Him. And I knew Him not: but He that sent me to baptize with water, He said unto me, Upon Whomsoever thou shalt see the Spirit descending, and abiding upon Him, the same is He that baptizeth with the Holy Spirit.*[2]

It is more than remarkable, it is almost startling to discover that the Gospels which chronicle the life and ministry of Christ, have no account of this baptism of the Spirit, save the prophecy of His coming uttered by John the Baptist, who spoke of it as something beyond himself, his message, and his age.

What the baptism of the Spirit is may be gathered from the word of the Master to Nicodemus: *Jesus answered, Verily, verily, I say unto thee, Except a man be born of water and the Spirit, he cannot enter into the kingdom of God.*[3] The inference is, that if a man be born of water and the Spirit, he can enter into the kingdom of God. But follow the words still further: *That which is born of the flesh is flesh; and that which is born of the Spirit is spirit. Marvel not that I said unto thee, Ye must be born anew. The wind bloweth where it listeth, and thou hearest the voice thereof, but knowest not whence it cometh, and whither it goeth: so is every one that is born of the Spirit.*

Except a man be born of water and the Spirit is a

[1] John i. 26, 27. [2] John i. 32, 33. [3] John iii. 5-8.

passage about which there is great diversity of opinion. The Master is here linking His own teaching and dispensation to the teaching and dispensation that is concluding with the mission of John. The water baptism is the baptism of John, and the Spirit baptism is the baptism of Jesus, the gift of life. That which is symbolized by the first is necessary, for repentance must precede life; but the baptism of the Spirit is the gift of life by which a man is admitted into the kingdom of God.

In the Gospels, John standing as the forerunner, declared: *I indeed baptize you with water; but there cometh He that is mightier than I . . . He shall baptize you with the Holy Spirit.*[1] Years passed, John's ministry was ended, the earthly ministry of Christ was ended, the Cross and Resurrection were accomplished facts. Jesus now stood amid His disciples, and before He ascended on high He said to them: *John indeed baptized with water; but ye shall be baptized with the Holy Spirit not many days hence.*[2] There had been as yet no baptism with the Holy Spirit; and, consequently, these men gathered around Christ had not yet entered into the final relationship with Him that characterizes the Christian dispensation, and forms the holy catholic Church. They had been the disciples of a Jewish Messiah; but now that relation was passing away, and the living Lord in resurrection glory was about to pour upon them the baptism predicted by John.

[1] Luke iii. 16. [2] Acts i. 5.

Christ took up the words of His forerunner, and claimed that they were to be fulfilled in the experience of these men: *John indeed baptized with water*—that is as far as they had gone at the moment; but the greater blessing was coming—*ye shall be baptized with the Holy Spirit not many days hence.*

And as I began to speak, the Holy Spirit fell on them, even as on us at the beginning. And I remembered the word of the Lord, how that He said, John indeed baptized with water; but ye shall be baptized with the Holy Spirit. If then God gave unto them the like gift as He did also unto us, when we believed on the Lord Jesus Christ, who was I, that I could withstand God?[1] Peter, in giving an account of the conversion of Cornelius, declared that these men were baptized with the Spirit when, as he preached, they believed on Christ. The teaching of both these passages evidently is, that the Spirit's baptism is that by which men pass into the new relationship. In both places a contrast is drawn between the baptism of the Spirit and the baptism of John, showing that the baptism of the Spirit was the power which took men beyond the legalism of the old dispensation into the vital relationship of the new.

Are ye ignorant that all we who were baptized into Christ Jesus were baptized into His death? We were buried therefore with Him through baptism into death: that like as Christ was raised from the dead through the

[1] Acts xi. 15-17.

glory of the Father, so we also might walk in newness of life.[1] This is the only direct reference to the baptism of the Spirit in the Letter to the Romans. Certainly the baptism referred to is the Spirit's baptism, for surely no man is baptized by water into the death of Christ. Water baptism may be a symbol of the great fact that a man has passed from death unto life, but the baptism by which men are actually brought into relationship with the death and the life of Christ is the baptism of the Spirit; and it is quite evident that in this argument of the Epistle a reference is made to the beginnings of spiritual life—to the initial blessing, to the blessing of regeneration.

For in[2] *one Spirit were we all baptized into one body, whether Jews or Greeks, whether bond or free.*[3] Here again the reference must be to the moment when men entered the Church of Christ; and the statement is that then they were baptized in the Holy Spirit.

For ye are all sons of God, through faith, in Christ Jesus. For as many of you as were baptized into Christ did put on Christ.[4] Faith was the condition of the baptism by which these people put on Christ and became sons of God, that baptism being, undoubtedly, the baptism of the Holy Spirit.

One Lord, one faith, one baptism, one God and Father of all.[5]

[1] Rom. vi. 3, 4. [2] Notice the slight alteration of the Revised Version—not *by one Spirit*. [3] 1 Cor. xii. 13. [4] Gal. iii. 26, 27. [5] Eph. iv. 5, 6.

One Lord—the object of the sinner's faith; *one faith*—centred upon the one Lord; *one baptism*—the baptism of the Holy Spirit, by which the sinner becomes the Lord's; *one God and Father*—the new relationship that God bears to the sinner when, baptized by the Spirit, he passes into the place of adoption. Here baptism takes its place at the beginning of the Christian life, immediately succeeding faith in the revealed Lord, and succeeded by the new relationship to God.

. . . *When the longsuffering of God waited in the days of Noah, while the ark was a preparing, wherein few, that is, eight souls, were saved through water: which also in the antitype doth now save you, even baptism, not the putting away of the filth of the flesh, but the interrogation of a good conscience toward God, through the resurrection of Jesus Christ.*[1]

Peter says that in the days of Noah the people were saved by water; and that men are saved to-day by that of which water is a figure—that is to say, men are saved by the baptism of the Holy Spirit.

This is a review of the whole of the passages in the New Testament that refer to the question of the baptism of the Spirit. In every case the reference is, not to some blessing subsequent to regeneration, but to regeneration itself—to that supernatural miracle by which a soul passes from darkness into light, out of death into life, from the thraldom of sin and Satan into the glorious liberty of a child of God.

[1] 1 Pet. iii. 20, 21 (margin).

This sweeps away the view that the baptism of the Spirit is a second blessing. There is absolutely no warrant in the whole teaching of Scripture for such view; and therefore there is, further, no warrant for the popular and prevalent idea that the Holy Spirit must be asked for, or waited for.

Referring to the oft-quoted words of the Master, *If ye then, being evil, know how to give good gifts unto your children, how much more shall your Father which is in heaven give good things to them that ask Him?*[1] it has already been shown[2] that these words were spoken while He was fulfilling His work as the Jewish Messiah to Jewish disciples. They never asked, and therefore never received the Spirit through their asking. He came in reply to the asking of Jesus, upon the ground of His finished work. The Spirit is never given in answer to human asking; but upon the ground of repentance and faith, man is baptized therewith, and from that moment the Spirit of God takes possession and dwells within. The believer may check Him, hinder Him, thwart Him, and grieve Him, but from the moment of the new birth he is a temple of the Holy Spirit. It is, then, in the initial miracle of regeneration that souls are baptized with the Holy Spirit.

On the same ground it is not right that Christian people should profess to be waiting for the baptism of the Spirit. The words, *Tarry, . . . until ye be clothed*

[1] Matt. vii. 11. [2] Chapter VII.

with power from on high,[1] have no application to new-born souls at all; or if they have an application, it is one that is a sad revelation of a condition of life that dishonours the Lord. If men have to tarry until endued with power, it is not because God has not given the Spirit, but because there is something in the life which will not let the Spirit work. Every believer is a temple of the Holy Spirit; and if there be tarrying, it is on account of some disobedience, and not on account of any unreadiness on the part of God to bestow full blessing upon all His children. Such tarrying is not the waiting of man for the Spirit, but the waiting of the Spirit for man.

There are certain passages in the Acts of the Apostles which are used to show that the gift of the Holy Spirit or the baptism of the Spirit is subsequent to conversion.

Philip went to Samaria and preached there; people believed in Jesus, and were baptized in His name. After that the apostles visited these believers, and they received the Holy Spirit. Therefore, it is asserted that people believe on Christ and are baptized; but the Holy Spirit has to be received as a second blessing.

Carefully notice what actually took place. Philip came to Samaria, preached in the name of Jesus, and men believed in some intellectual sense, and were baptized. Among the number was Simon Magus. It is impossible to distinguish between Simon Magus and the rest, because the statement that Simon Magus believed

[1] Luke xxiv. 49.

is as distinct as is the statement that the others did so, and the Scriptures as distinctly state that he was baptized because he believed, as that the others were baptized because they believed. But when the apostles came, Peter thus described Simon Magus: *Thou hast neither part nor lot in this matter: for thy heart is not right before God. . . . For I see that thou art in the gall of bitterness and in the bond of iniquity.*[1] As to the others, Peter unfolded to them the full meaning of the Gospel message, and those that heard it received the Holy Spirit. None of them had received the Spirit, and therefore none of them were born again. These people of Samaria, it must be remembered, held the Jewish view of Messiahship, and their belief in Jesus, was in Him as having come for the establishment of the earthly kingdom. They had given an intellectual assent to the story of Jesus, and, having believed it, had consented to go through an outward form and ceremony; but not until the apostles came, and the Spirit of God fell upon them, were they members of the Church or converted souls.

Again, the story of the conversion of Saul of Tarsus is used in the same way: *And Ananias departed, and entered into the house; and laying his hands on him said, Brother Saul, the Lord, even Jesus, Who appeared unto thee in the way which thou camest, hath sent me, that thou mayest receive thy sight, and be filled with the*

[1] Acts viii. 21-23.

Holy Spirit. And straightway there fell from his eyes as it were scales, and he received his sight; and he arose and was baptized; and he took food and was strengthened.[1] Concerning this case there is certainly room for doubt. The probability, however, is that the procedure is in harmony with all the rest, and that Saul was arrested and convinced of the kingship of Jesus on the road to Damascus, but did not enter into the Church by regeneration until the fuller light came from the instruction of Ananias. Even if it be granted that there were certain people who believed in Jesus, yet did not immediately receive the Holy Spirit, it must be remembered that cases like these are not to be found in the subsequent story of the Acts.

The passage most often used in this way is the question Paul addressed to certain people at Ephesus: *Did ye receive the Holy Spirit when ye believed?*[2] The Authorized Version, with less accuracy, translated it: *Have ye received the Holy Spirit since ye believed?* This, it is alleged, gives a clear case of people who had believed and yet had not received the Holy Spirit. But here again the facts of the case must be carefully examined. Paul came to Ephesus, and found there a little company of believers in Jesus. There is no record as to why he put this question to them, but he asked them: *Did ye receive the Holy Spirit when ye believed?* The question evidently carries with it the thought that they

[1] Acts ix. 17-19. [2] Acts xix. 2.

ought to have done so. *And they said unto him, Nay, we did not so much as hear whether the Holy Spirit was given. And he said* [most probably in surprise], *Into what then were ye baptized? And they said, Into John's baptism. And Paul said, John baptized with the baptism of repentance, saying unto the people, that they should believe on Him which should come after him, that is, on Jesus. And when they heard this, they were baptized into the name of the Lord Jesus. And when Paul had laid his hands upon them, the Holy Spirit came on them.*[1]

These people were not Christians, they were not born again; they were the disciples of Jesus as He was heralded by John. It was therefore necessary for them to receive the Holy Spirit, in order that they might pass from that region of water baptism into the region of the baptism of the Holy Spirit. But it may be wondered how there came to be disciples of John as far away as Ephesus. The explanation is found in the context: *Now a certain Jew named Apollos, an Alexandrian by race, a learned man, came to Ephesus; and he was mighty in the Scriptures. . . . Being fervent in spirit, he spake and taught carefully the things concerning Jesus, knowing only the baptism of John.*[2] That accounts for the presence of disciples at Ephesus. When Apollos came there, he himself did not know the baptism of the Spirit; and these were people baptized with

[1] Acts xix. 2-6. [2] Acts xviii. 24, 25.

the baptism of John, and knowing therefore only so much of Jesus as John himself had been able to declare. Apollos himself had to be instructed in *the way of God more carefully;*[1] and when the apostle came, this handful of believers in John's baptism had also to be taught. Therefore to interpret this text as teaching that beyond the day of conversion there is some other gift of the Holy Spirit necessary, is to wrest it out of its proper setting and to set up a new standard of Christian life, for which it gives no warrant.

There are many moral people who admire Christ, and have perchance even been baptized with John's baptism, but they have never been born again: to them this text has a direct application. But to people born again of the Spirit of God, there can be no application of this message, because by the new birth they have received the Holy Spirit, and into that Spirit they have been baptized.

The baptism of the Spirit, then, is that miracle of regeneration whereby a man passes into the new realm of life in which Christ is supreme in the power of His own communicated life.

In the great commission, *He that believeth and is baptized shall be saved; but he that disbelieveth shall be condemned,*[2] most assuredly the baptism referred to is that of the Holy Spirit. The words declare the condition of salvation and the promise thereof: *He that be-*

[1] Acts xviii. 26. [2] Mark xvi. 16.

lieveth [that is the human condition] *and is baptized* [that is the Divine miracle] *shall be saved.* When the negative side is stated, baptism is omitted, as being unnecessary; for he that disbelieveth cannot be baptized. If it is water baptism, he can; but if it is the baptism of the Spirit, he cannot. Thus in that commission the Lord most evidently puts the baptism of the Spirit at the very entrance of the kingdom. Men believing (one faith), and being baptized (one baptism), are saved; while he that believeth not is condemned.

By this baptism of the Spirit the individual becomes a temple of the Holy Spirit; and the message that ought to be delivered to Christian people to-day is: *Ye are a temple of God,*[1] do not desecrate the temple, but let the Divine One Who indwells, govern absolutely the whole being. Not that the heart should be opened to admit the Spirit; for God's children are such because the Holy Spirit has already taken possession, and even though defiled, they nevertheless are the temples of the Holy Spirit; for it was not to sanctified people, in the usually accepted sense of the term, that the apostle said: *Ye are a temple of God.* The central fact, the great and almost appalling miracle of Christianity, is that persons baptized by the Spirit become temples of God. They also become members of the catholic Church, parts of the Body of Christ. Moreover, by that baptism they are sealed unto a consummation, sealed unto the final day of redemption.

[1] Cor. iii. 16.

It is to be feared that many, in emphasizing what is spoken of as the second blessing—an idea and an expression to be found nowhere in Scripture—insult and degrade the blessing of regeneration, which holds within itself all subsquent unfoldings of blessing and of power.

XVI

THE FILLING OF THE SPIRIT

(THE NEW TESTAMENT IDEAL)

IN discussing this subject, the one matter of importance is the discovery of the sense in which the term *the filling of the Spirit* is used in the New Testament.

In one form or another it occurs four times prior to the Pentecostal effusion:—

For he shall be great in the sight of the Lord, and he shall drink no wine nor strong drink; and he shall be filled with the Holy Spirit, even from his mother's womb.[1]

And it came to pass, when Elisabeth heard the salutation of Mary, the babe leaped in her womb; and Elisabeth was filled with the Holy Spirit; and she lifted up her voice with a loud cry.[2]

And his father Zacharias was filled with the Holy Spirit, and prophesied, saying.[3]

And Jesus, full of the Holy Spirit, returned from the Jordan, and was led by the Spirit in the wilderness during forty days.[4]

[1] Luke i. 15. [2] Luke i. 41, 42. [3] Luke i. 67. [4] Luke iv. 1.

John, the forerunner of the Christ, was filled with the Spirit from his birth. Elisabeth was filled with the Spirit for the singing of a sacred song. Zacharias was filled with the Spirit for the uttering of prophecy. The Lord was filled with the Spirit for the exercise of His Messianic ministry.

This filling of certain persons, prior to the Pentecostal effusion, was a continuation of the Spirit's work, in keeping with the methods which had characterized the whole of the dispensation then drawing to a close. Just as in the past the Spirit had filled men for the accomplishment of special work for God; so, as the dispensation drew to a close, and Messiah approached, He again equipped those who were to do the special work the occasion demanded.

A clear line is drawn between the old and the new dispensations; and the teaching of the New Testament concerning the filling of the Spirit in the dispensation which had its birth at Pentecost is very distinct.

The expression occurs in the Acts of the Apostles eight times, and once in the Letter to the Ephesians. These passages practically contain the whole system.

The sum of that teaching is that the Spirit-filled life is the normal condition of the believer. There are those who believe that the filling of the Spirit is something which is not merely a *second blessing* in the experience of the majority of Christians, but in the purpose of God. But just as the baptism of the Spirit is never spoken of as a second blessing, but always as the initial blessing of regeneration; so in the economy of God the filling of the Spirit is coincident with conversion. When a man is baptized with the Spirit, he is born of the Spirit, and is filled with the Spirit. There are many who do not enter into the realization of that blessedness at conversion. In the purpose of God, however, the normal condition of Christian life is that of being baptized by the Spirit into life, and filled with the Spirit for life.

Nothing can be clearer than the statement of what happened on the Day of Pentecost: *And there appeared unto them tongues parting asunder, like as of fire; and it sat upon each one of them. And they were all filled with the Holy Spirit, and began to speak with other tongues, as the Spirit gave them utterance.*[1] In the moment when the group of Jewish disciples was transformed into the Church, the Spirit was not only given to them, He filled them. It is evident, therefore, from the account of the opening of the dispensation, that in the purpose of God those who passed into its new life, new glory, new breadth, and new beauty were baptized and filled with the Spirit.

An illustration of this occurs in the history of the early days. Saul of Tarsus, *breathing threatening and slaughter against the disciples of the Lord,*[2] was on his way to Damascus, when he was suddenly arrested by the shining of a light from heaven; he heard the voice of

[1] Acts ii. 3, 4. [2] Acts ix. 1.

Jesus, and yielded to the claim of the Master, saying: *What shall I do, Lord?*[1] He remained blind; and having been led to Damascus, the Master sent Ananias to him: *And Ananias departed, and entered into the house; and laying his hands on him, said, Brother Saul, the Lord even Jesus, who appeared unto thee in the way which thou camest, hath sent me, that thou mayest receive thy sight, and be filled with the Holy Spirit.*[2] It may be a matter of opinion as to whether that was the moment of his conversion or not.[3] Even if he were born of the Spirit on the way to Damascus, the filling of the Spirit, according to this teaching, came immediately, and was part of the very earliest experience of his Christian life.

It follows, therefore, that the will of God for His people is that they should be filled at once; that God does not give a man the Spirit to-day, and then make him, as a necessity, wait for perhaps a number of years before he is filled with the Spirit; but that the supreme miracle by which a man is born of the Spirit, and so baptized of the Spirit into new relationship with Christ, is also the miracle by which he becomes filled with the Spirit of God.

There is another use made of this same phrase in the Acts of the Apostles: *And when they had set them in the midst, they inquired, By what power, or in what name, have ye done this? Then Peter, filled with the Holy Spirit, said unto them, Ye rulers of the people, and*

[1] Acts xxii. 10. [2] Acts ix. 17. [3] Chapter XV.

elders, if we this day are examined. . . .[1] The sense of the word *filled* in this case is that of being specially filled for special work. It does not describe a normal condition of life, but a specific filling, in order that he might be specially prepared for work that awaited him at that moment. Filled with the Spirit, he spake the words.

Another instance of the same kind is chronicled in the words: *But Saul, who is also called Paul, filled with the Holy Spirit, fastened his eyes on him* [that is, on Elymas the sorcerer], *and said, O full of all guile and all villany, thou son of the devil, thou enemy of all righteousness, wilt thou not cease to pervert the right ways of the Lord?*[2] A special work of discipline had to be performed: a man who had wronged the truth and the faith had to be rebuked, and Paul was suddenly filled with the Holy Spirit for the doing of that particular work.

Again the term is used in a way that includes the filling for life and service, the former being viewed as the condition for the latter: *Look ye out therefore, brethren, from among you seven men of good report, full of the Spirit and of wisdom, whom we may appoint over this business. . . . And the saying pleased the whole multitude: and they chose Stephen, a man full of faith and of the Holy Spirit, and Philip. . . .*[3] These men were chosen for work in the Church because they were full of the Spirit.

[1] Acts iv. 7-9. [2] Acts xiii. 9, 10. [3] Acts vi. 3-5.

It is written of Barnabas that *he was a good man, and full of the Holy Spirit and of faith: and much people was added unto the Lord.*[1]

These are the occasions where the term is used in the Acts of the Apostles with reference to service. Twice in the case of the deacons, and also in the case of Barnabas, it is evident that the condition for service is that men should be full of the Spirit—not that there should be a special gift, but that they should be living the life that is Spirit-filled. Where that is so, they are fit for the office of deacon; where that is so, they are fit, as was Barnabas, for visiting the churches and for administering spiritual comfort. But from the other instances of Peter and Paul, it is equally clear that the term is used with reference to a special filling for a special work.

The phrase is also used in a sense proving that though the filling of the Spirit is the normal condition of the believer's life, yet it may be lost and restored: *And when they had prayed, the place was shaken wherein they were gathered together*; and they were all filled *with the Holy Spirit, and they spake the word of God with boldness.*[2] This has been erroneously spoken of as *the second Pentecost.* There can be no second Pentecost. Pentecost came once and for ever. Undoubtedly a second manifestation of the Spirit is here referred to; but it was rendered necessary because these men had passed into a realm of fear and of trembling. Peter and

[1] Acts xi. 24. [2] Acts iv. 31.

John were imprisoned, and the disciples were gathered in fear and trembling, hardly daring to open the doors or show themselves. When Peter and John were miraculously restored and came into their midst, they gave themselves to prayer, asking that they might have boldness. The answer to their prayer was the shaking of the house in which they were assembled, and their refilling with the Spirit. These men had not lost the Spirit. They had been sealed unto the day of redemption. Born of the Spirit, the Spirit remained in them; but through their own fear, unbelief, and lack of loyalty to Jesus Christ, the blessing of the Spirit's fulness had been lost. When they returned to the Lord, the filling was granted to them anew.

Another instance is recorded which gives yet another light on the subject. Of Stephen it is said: *But he, being full of the Holy Spirit, looked up stedfastly into heaven, and saw the glory of God, and Jesus standing on the right hand of God.*[1] Passing through martyrdom, Stephen was strengthened in his suffering by a vision of his Master in the glory. The condition for seeing the vision was the fulness of the Holy Spirit.

These are the only instances in the Acts of the Apostles where the term *filling of the Spirit* is used. The sum of their teaching may thus be stated. The Spirit-filled life is the normal condition of the believer; it may be lost; it can be restored. New-born

[1] Acts vii. 55.

souls, baptized by the Spirit into union with Christ, are filled; but very often, for lack of clear teaching and full understanding of the law of the Spirit, the fulness of the blessing is lost.

There are thousands whose memories go back to some convention, to some service, to some hour of loneliness with God, when they became Spirit-filled in a sense which they had never experienced before. The explanation of this fact is, that at some point in their Christian life, preceding the experience of which they speak as a *second blessing,* they had been disobedient to the Divine purpose; and therefore the blame of the low-level life preceding that blessing is to be laid, not upon the economy of God, but upon the disloyalty of the believer. There is no reason why a man should not immediately from the moment of regeneration enter into all the blessedness of the Spirit-filled life: that is the Divine intention, and that is the Divine purpose. This is a question of condition and not of finality. The law of growth is that the believer should be Spirit-filled.

For special service there is, however, a special filling of the Holy Spirit, and whether it be Peter or Paul or any other servant of Christ having a special work to do for Him, that servant may be especially filled with the Spirit for the accomplishment of that special work.

There is one other passage demanding attention: *And be not drunken with wine, wherein is riot, but be filled with the Spirit.*[1] The injunction *be filled with the Spirit* is in the imperative. It is a command; and the fact that it is a command lays responsibility, not upon God, but upon the believer. In the commencement of the Epistle the whole scheme of thought which was here in the mind of the apostle is stated: *In Whom ye also, having heard the word of the truth, the gospel of your salvation,—in Whom, having also believed, ye were sealed with the Holy Spirit of promise, which is an earnest of our inheritance.*[2] The sealing of the Spirit is identical with the baptism of the Spirit. The apostle is writing to people who are sealed with the Spirit, and he charges them to be filled with the Spirit. Here are two distinct things—the sealing of the Spirit, and the filling of the Spirit. Though the filling be coincident with the sealing, it is necessary to enjoin these people to be filled, because that is the point of their responsibility. That responsibility is revealed in the words: *Grieve not the Holy Spirit of God, in Whom ye were sealed unto the day of redemption.*[3] Here is a solution of the mystery that gathers around the experience of thousands of Christians. They are born of the Spirit, and none will deny that they are Christians. They are not, however, filled with the Spirit, for the fruit of the Spirit is not manifest in their lives. The reason for this is that they have grieved the Holy Spirit of God somewhere in the past. The path of obedience has been

[1] Eph. v. 18. [2] Eph. i, 13, 14. [3] Eph. iv. 30.

clearly marked, and they have disobeyed. Christian people who are baptized by the Spirit into new relationship with Christ have grieved the Spirit by disobedience, lukewarmness, indifference to the claims of Christ, worldliness, or frivolity, and they are therefore not filled with the Spirit. The subject of responsibility, showing what are the conditions of the filling and what is the result of the filling, will form the subject of a subsequent chapter.[1]

Dr. Erdmann, of Philadelphia, has given a formula of the law of the Spirit in these words—*One baptism, many fillings;* and perhaps no statement of the case could be more helpful. It is borne out by New Testament teaching and history. One baptism—the moment of the new birth, when the Spirit comes upon the repenting and believing soul and unites that soul to Christ. Christians may be disobedient and lose the filling of the Spirit, and by repentance and obedience it may be restored; and in the experience of multitudes of believers this formula is proved to be correct—One baptism, but many fillings.

This is also illustrated, as has been already shown, by the filling of the apostles at the baptism of Pentecost, and by their refilling subsequently, which was by no means a second baptism. The specific fillings for service are the fillings to overflowing, of which the Lord Himself declared: *He that believeth on Me . . . out of*

[1] Chapter XIX.

his belly shall flow rivers of living water.[1] This third phase of blessing, the specific work of the Spirit for service, has sometimes been spoken of as an anointing of the Spirit, but without Scripture warrant. The term *anointing of the Spirit*[2] is used only twice with regard to Christians. In both places the reference is to regeneration. There are those who are perpetually declaring that Christians must follow in the steps of Christ, and that, as He was anointed for His work, so must they be for theirs; but there is no perfect analogy between the dealings of God with Christ, and His dealings with believers, because Christ was sinless and spotless, while they have always to be dealt with as those who have failed, and must be restored to the divine pattern. It would be just as incorrect to speak of a second anointing as of a second Pentecost, or of a second Pentecost as of a second anointing. The anointing which is on the child of God is that which was received at regeneration. What is needed for life is the perpetual filling of the Spirit which is the normal condition of those who are living in the way of God, and the specific fillings to overflowing which may always be counted on when special service demands.

Every believer on the Lord Jesus Christ having vital relationship with Him, became a Christian when baptized with the Holy Spirit, and at the moment of baptism was filled with the Spirit. If not filled with the

[1] John vii. 38. [2] 2 Cor. i. 21. 1 John ii. 27.

Spirit now, the blame is to be laid, not upon the Master, but upon personal disobedience. Somewhere in the life of relationship to Christ there was a moment of disobedience, a moment of disloyalty, a moment of rebellion against government; and by that rebellion the filling of the Spirit was lost. It may be restored by restoration to obedience, the new yielding of the life to the Spirit. He will enter and will take possession of the territory from which by disobedience He has been excluded. Dr. Handley Moule, who is perhaps one of the most lucid exponents of the Scriptures upon this subject, says that the difference between a soul that is filled with the Spirit and one that is unfilled, is the difference between a well in which there is a spring of water choked, and a well from which the obstruction has been removed, so that the water springs up and fills the well. In every child of God the Spirit is present, waiting to fill; and if He does not fill the whole life to its utmost bound with His own energy, light, and power, it is because there is something which prevents Him, and which must be removed before He can do His blessed work.

The filling of the Spirit is indeed an experience far beyond that of which the majority of Christians know anything; but it is the purpose of God that every child of His should be filled, not a year, nor two years, nor ten years after conversion, but at the moment of conversion, and perpetually until the consummation of his sojourn upon the earth.

XVII

THE POWER OF THE SPIRIT

THE first chapter of the Acts of the Apostles is of great interest, as giving the last glimpse of the disciples of Jesus apart from the indwelling of the Holy Spirit. The picture is full of instruction, revealing with clearness the enormous difference there must ever be between man in his fallen nature, and man as he may be through the baptism and indwelling of the Spirit. One cannot look at this picture, incomplete though it may be, without seeing that these men were still ignorant and selfish. There is no comparison between the men of the first chapter, and the men of the subsequent history contained in the book.

They came to the risen Lord with the old question: *Lord, dost Thou at this time restore the kingdom to Israel?*[1] They had made no progress. The events of the past weeks had not been sufficient to reveal to them the great essential verities of the Christian faith. They were still bound by the materialism of Judaism; the

[1] Acts i. 6.

spiritual vision had not yet fallen upon them; they did not understand the mission of Christ. They were still looking for a temporal kingdom which should be immediately set up. They had no appreciation of the fact that Jesus was passing to a hidden throne and a hidden crown, and that the work to which they were now to be committed was not temporal, external, and material, but eternal, internal, and spiritual.

They had not yet escaped from the narrow national prejudices which had been the curse of the nation for so long. *Dost Thou at this time restore the kingdom to Israel?* They had no idea of the world-wide kingdom of the Messiah. Their vision was still limited by the horizon of their own people. The Master had ever looked beyond the confines of the nation. Not so the disciples, neither were they yet able to do so.

They did not understand that the work He had come to do was something absolutely new. They dreamed of the restoration of the old. *Restore* was the word they made use of.

Their love was deep, and true, and intense; their knowledge during the days of discipleship was far in advance of that of the men of their age; the Resurrection was to them a fact, for the living Christ was in their midst. Yet they were absolutely unfit for the work they had to do, for they were still looking for the temporal kingdom to be set up in the same way that other earthly kingdoms had been.

To these men Christ said: *Ye shall receive power, when the Holy Spirit is come upon you: and ye shall be My witnesses both in Jerusalem, and in all Judæa and Samaria, and unto the uttermost part of the earth.*[1] This word answers and corrects the false idea contained in their question. They said: *Dost Thou at this time restore the kingdom?* They thought of a return to old things. He replied: *Ye shall be My witnesses.* He directed their thought to the new Centre. They said: *Dost Thou at this time restore the kingdom?* Their minds were fixed upon earthly things. He said: *Ye shall receive power, when the Holy Spirit is come.* His mind encompassed the spiritual relationship. They said: *Dost Thou at this time restore the kingdom to Israel?* They were bound by the idea of the nation. He replied: *Jerusalem, and in all Judæa and Samaria, and unto the uttermost part of the earth.* He included the world in His vision.

This was a new beginning, moving out from Himself as Centre, having the Holy Spirit as Administrator, and the disciples as channels of communication.

There is a sense in which these words of the Master cannot be addressed to Christian people to-day. These men had not yet been baptized with the Holy Spirit; they were not yet born again. Those that are Christians to-day are such by that baptism and new birth; and, consequently, they possess the power promised to these men.

[1] Acts i. 8.

The central principle declared is that fitness for service in the new covenant lies within the realm of the power of the Holy Spirit. This is of perpetual application, and it is therefore important that a chapter should be devoted to its consideration. There are three matters to be noted: first, the power needed; secondly, the nature of the power available; and, thirdly, the purpose for which the power is bestowed.

For the accomplishment of their work these men needed a fourfold force. They needed intellectual power, because of their ignorance and inability to appreciate the meaning of the Master's mission. They needed spiritual power, in the sense of ability to do righteously, notwithstanding the carnal possibilities still resident in their own lives. They needed a new power of the affection and will, because of the tremendous forces which would be arrayed against them in the prosecution of the work that was before them. They needed power for the accomplishment of the results at which they aimed, because the forces hitherto used in great movements would be denied them.

It is not necessary to deal at length with the first phase of this need, having already referred to it; but their lack of understanding of the Cross must be remembered. The apostle in writing to the Corinthians described the Cross as being *unto Jews a stumbling-block*[1] —that is, something in the way, an obstruction; and up to this point their outlook was purely Jewish. Think

[1] 1 Cor. i. 23.

how they had followed the Master, and how they had learned to love Him. Then remember how swiftly doom fell upon Him, their Teacher, their Friend. They had seen Him overcome by the detested Roman power, and nailed to the Cross. It is only as their place is occupied in imagination, and the prejudices of their birth and education are in some measure understood, that it will be possible to appreciate how completely the Cross must have extinguished hope for them, and how sincere and sad was the sigh of the men who walked to Emmaus: *We hoped that it was He which should redeem Israel.*[1]

Of the mysteries that are the essential grandeur of Christianity,—death, the entrance to life—life won through death; defeat, the way into victory—victory won through defeat; darkness, the price of light—light dawning out of darkness,—they had no appreciation. They saw only the death, the defeat, and the darkness. The Cross was to them a stumbling-block. Afterwards they told the story of the Cross as being the story of love, of liberty, of light; but before they were able to do this, they needed a new intellectual grasp upon the things of God. The power they were to receive, after that the Holy Spirit came upon them was the new power of intelligence, enabling them to comprehend the true meaning of the facts they were to publish.

The second phase of the need is the power for holy

[1] Luke xxiv. 21.

living. In the purpose of God the force and meaning of the Cross were to be revealed to men not merely by the words of His servant's lips, but also by the transformation of their lives. Man had been the slave of his own carnality, dominated by the evil forces within him. Henceforth he is to be free from this power; in union with Jesus Christ he is to be master of the things that have mastered him. The essential message of the Gospel is the declaration that through the Cross and Resurrection of Christ a new dynamic is at the disposal of men, in the power of which they may be victorious, trampling under their feet the lust of which hitherto they have been the slaves. Witness to this truth is to be borne not only by a testimony of the lips, but by the triumph of lives, proving the accuracy of the testimony. First, a clear appreciation of the meaning of the Cross; secondly, the personal apprehension of its power; behind the testimony the triumph—the testimony proved by the triumph, the triumph accounted for by the testimony. Such is the Divine ideal of the work that lay before these men. If this indeed be true, it is evident that they needed this power of Holiness that their lives might be transformed. It is this power that He promised to them when He spoke of the coming of the Holy Spirit.

Further, they needed new power of the affection and will. Persecution awaited them. All the forces that had been against their Master would oppose them. The doctrine of deliverance which they were to announce was revolutionary, and the powers that held men in slavery would array themselves to silence their voices and stop their progress. If they were to continue bearing witness to Him through darkness as well as through light, when the way was rough as well as when it was smooth, through the perils of popularity as well as through the dangers of ostracism, they needed some new power of the affection and the will, which should make their love burn as a flame, and set their faces as flint.

They had already been in one place of testing, and with what dire results! Oh the tragedy of that simple sentence. *They all left Him, and fled!*[1] If they had done that while He was yet with them, while the power of His personality was upon them, how would they act when the clouds had hidden Him from view and the sound of His voice was not to be heard? They stood in need of a power that should keep love burning, and the will to accomplish their work unconquered.

They cannot drive the world
Until themselves be driven.

This power is precisely what Jesus promised in the indwelling Spirit. Ever revealing the fact of the Christ to the disciples, He would capture the soul by the vision of love every moment, and make the will to do His work invincible as the very will of God.

[1] Mark xiv. 50.

Once more, they needed a new working power. Said the Master: *Ye shall be My witnesses both in Jerusalem, and in all Judæa and Samaria, and unto the uttermost part of the earth.*[1] They were to tell the story of His life and death to all men; they were to urge His claims upon the attention of men; they were to win men for Him. And all this was to be done without the aids that human wisdom would immediately think of. The conquests of the past had been the conquests of argument, and policy, and the sword. These were all denied them. They had no commission to persuade men by argument. Policy had no place in their programme. Of the sword the Master Himself had said: *Put up . . . thy sword . . . for all they that take the sword shall perish with the sword.*[2]

By other methods they were to accomplish their work. The propagandists of the new kingdom were sent forth in the name of an absent King, with no sign of power recognized by the men of the world. They needed some new power, and this is exactly what the Master promised them when He spoke of the coming of the Holy Spirit. Having that power, they should pass into all lands, and do deeds and win triumphs more mighty and marvellous than any that the world had ever seen or known.

So far the first disciples have been under consideration, but the teaching is permanent. No man can do the work of God until he have the Holy Spirit, and is

[1] Acts i. 8. [2] Matt. xxvi. 52.

endued with power. It is impossible to preach the Gospel save in the power of the Spirit, because none can comprehend the true meaning of the Cross of Christ unless taught by the Spirit of God. Neither a knowledge of the letter of the New Testament, nor a system of theology, is sufficient to equip for preaching the Cross. Nothing short of the immediate, direct, personal illumination of the Spirit is sufficient equipment. Witness for the Master is impossible save to those who co-operate with the supreme Witness. The keenest intellect and the most cultured mind are unable to understand the mystery of redemption, and therefore cannot explain it to others. Whoever can say light has broken upon the Cross and the eternal morning has dawned, is able to do so through the direct illumination of the Holy Spirit; and apart from that, there can be no witness and no service.

It is equally true that there can be no witness in the life but by this constant indwelling of the Holy Spirit. The nature is still capable of sin; and if it pass from under the Divine government, all manner of evil will follow. Men can only live the life that is in harmony with the teaching of Christ as they are possessed and energized by the Holy Spirit of God.

It is also necessary that the affection and will should be under the dominion of the Spirit. Perpetual love and perennial joy are only possible where the Spirit of God abides at the centre of being, energizing the will that else would fail, and strengthening every step in the path of obedience. Save as the life is lived under the dominion of the Spirit, temptation will prove too strong and the sacred Name will be dishonoured.

Again, in all service for God, the power of the Spirit is still needed. Much has been done since the apostolic days for making the work of the preacher easy. The Canon of the New Testament is complete; theology has been systematized; the necessity for the thorough equipment of the preacher educationally, wherever possible, is realized: these and many other advantages which the early Christian preachers had not, contribute to the smoothness of the pathway of the preacher to-day. All these, however, are insufficient. Beside them all, and as the power which alone makes them of real use, the Holy Spirit must equip the preacher, or preaching will degenerate into lifeless rhetoric, or heartless argument. This is equally true of every form of Christian service. It is pre-eminently the day of organization. Societies have multiplied on every hand, and the machinery of the Church is complex and multitudinous. This is all cause for thankfulness, but it cannot too often be repeated, that apart from the Holy Spirit's control and direction, all is dead. The advantages of the moment are not to be despised. Those who would go back to primitive simplicity must deny the guidance of God in the centuries. Let all be yielded to the fire and power of the Spirit for cleansing and energy, and the pulpit will be the greatest force in all human life, and every organization of the Church will throb and pulsate with Divine energy.

The nature of the power is evident. It is the coming of God to man for the accomplishment of a Divine purpose in this sacred partnership. Man is helpless apart from this immediate co-operation with God. God chooses to be helpless apart from co-operation with man. Within the next thirty years from Pentecost the whole known world was influenced by this handful of men who had been gathered by Jesus, and taught by Him with such matchless patience and gentleness, preparatory to the Spirit's baptism. Yet the world failed to comprehend the meaning or to explain the mystery of this new movement. The younger Pliny, in a letter to the Emperor about the Christians, said that after enquiries he found that they sang hymns about One called Jesus, and that they paid the taxes. A most excellent testimony. May it still be borne concerning all those who take the name of Christ! Yet what a remarkable analysis for an educated mind to offer! It was simple and sublime,—simple, in that it revealed his failure to comprehend the deep meaning of Christianity and his inability to do more than read the externals; sublime, in that it unintentionally, yet surely revealed the fact that joy and righteousness resulted from the worship of God in Christ, and the characters of men were so transformed that they sang and paid taxes. As a rule human nature is hardly capable of doing these things; but these men accomplished it, because righteousness itself had become a joy in the power of the name of Jesus. It is not to be wondered at that they were not understood. The usual signs of power were absent altogether. These people had no visible Head. The Founder had perished by the ignominious death of the Cross. They were gathered and marshalled and led, not to arming and battle by the cry of a warrior, but silently and surely, to the undermining of empires, and the downfall of dynasties. This element of mystery lasts until this hour. The man of the world is still unable to account for it. Proof of this is to be found in a perusal of his magazine articles occasionally. The secret of it all is, that within the Church, because within every individual member thereof, God has taken up His abode; and in a perpetual comradeship and co-operation He moves on towards the purposes of His heart, through all the forces that oppose, and the obstacles that hinder. Wherever Christianity has been a real force, working to success, it is because it has been spiritual. The wheels of the chariot are clogged by all attempts to make arrangements to help God. They are speeded when, self forgotten, the Spirit that indwells is permitted to have unquestioned and absolute control.

Yet let it be remembered that, if the force of Christianity is not of man, it operates through man. God has so chosen to work. This was symbolized on the Day of Pentecost by the cloven tongues of fire: *There appeared unto them tongues parting asunder, like as of fire; and it sat upon each one of them.*[1] *Tongues,* diversities of gifts; *fire,* the one Spirit. *Tongues,* the human instrument; *fire,* the Divine energy. Man the instrument; God, the Worker.

Much of the lack of power in service to-day is due to the fact that the true conception of what service should be has been lost. The only reason that those who are born again of the Spirit are left in the world is that they may be His witnesses. Paul distinctly teaches in his Letter to the Ephesians that the supreme vocation of the Church lies not in the present age nor in present circumstances. Her final work will be the manifestation of the wisdom and the grace of God to principalities and powers in the heavenly places. The reason why the Church is not at once removed to this higher service is, that in the midst of the darkness and death around, she may witness to her absent but living Lord.

Light is thrown upon this work by a consideration of the word *witness.* The word actually used is *martyr.* This word is used to-day almost exclusively of those who suffer persecution for the truth. That use of the word, while dignifying it, is in danger of obscuring its first intention. A martyr is one, convinced of truth, manifesting that truth in life. The fires of persecution never made martyrs—they revealed them. A man who was not already a martyr never laid down his life for

[1] Acts ii. 3.

truth. The noble army of martyrs died, not to become martyrs, but because they were martyrs. This is the distinctive service of all believers in this age. They are to reveal in transformed and transfigured lives the glory and beauty of the teaching and character of Jesus Christ. This ideal of service flings men back at once into the place of conscious dependence upon the Holy Spirit, for none can witness of Christ save in actual co-operation with Him. Two simple sentences will be helpful in order to understand the law of that co-operation:—

The Holy Spirit witnesses of Jesus only.
Only the Holy Spirit witnesses of Jesus.

It is very important to remember the first of these. The Spirit has nothing to say of Himself. His whole mission and message has to do with Christ. Many people to-day are waiting for a manifestation of the Spirit Himself. They are doomed to disappointment. When He obtains full possession of any individual, it is not His own Person and personality He makes real, but that of Jesus.

The second point is of equal importance. Everything that is known of the Saviour is known as the result of the illumination of the Holy Spirit. He is the Revealer of the Revealer. There can be no communication with Jesus until the Spirit reveals Him to the heart. There is no vision of the loveliness of His face save as the Spirit anoints the eyes. Herein lies the blessedness of this

Pentecostal age. The power for witnessing is the birthright of every believer. The Spirit reveals Christ to the consciousness. This new sense of the Master captivates the will and transforms the entire being into likeness to Himself. This development of character is also increased capacity for the reception of revelation. To that increased capacity the Spirit is able to make still more glorious revelation, which yet further increases capacity, and prepares the way for still more glorious revelation. Thus, in a proportionately increasing ratio, life under the control of the Spirit is manifesting the glory of the Master, and thus witnessing for Him.

For such witnessing the world waits to-day. Humanity amid its sobbing, and its sighing, needs a manifestation of the sons and daughters of the King; and in proportion as the temples of the Spirit are yielded to the Spirit, that great need of the race is being met.

BOOK VII

THE PRACTICAL APPLICATION

Breathe on me, Breath of God,
Fill me with life anew,
That I may love what Thou dost love,
And do what Thou wouldst do.

Breathe on me, Breath of God,
Until my heart is pure,
Until with Thee I will one will,
To do and to endure.

Breathe on me, Breath of God,
Blend all my soul with Thine,
Until this earthly part of me
Glows with Thy fire Divine.

Breathe on me, Breath of God,
So shall I never die,
But live with Thee the perfect life
Of Thine eternity.

E. Hatch.

XVIII

YE MUST BE BORN ANEW

NO person can be a child of God but by the renewing work of the Holy Spirit. The entrance to Christianity is perpetually and jealously guarded by the words of Jesus to Nicodemus: *Ye must be born anew.*[1] The reason for this is to be found in the very nature of Christianity. It presents an ideal of life, and enunciates an ethical code, of such a nature as to demand something more than themselves. Its ideal is Jesus. Its code of ethics is His teaching. These are united in a sacred and wondrous union, for all He taught men to be, He was Himself. So wondrous was He in beauty of character, and so searching and severe in the requirements of His law, that man in his impotence is absolutely unable to copy the one, or to obey the other. If Christianity, therefore, has nothing more to offer men than these, it is an impossible and impracticable ideal, a mere mirage of the desert, suggesting growth and fertility, but ever eluding the grasp of those

[1] John iii. 7.

who, weary and desolate, stretch out longing hands after its fruits. The something more required is the essential gift and power of Christianity. It comes to men with life which is the very life of the Ideal, and is therefore the dynamic of obedience to the code. Nothing short of actual participation in that life constitutes any human being a Christian. Admiration of the Person and character of Christ, together with patronage of His teaching, are insufficient, and indeed do but insult the purpose of Christianity, whose mission it is, not so much to captivate the admiration, as to remake and beautify the character.

These words of Jesus to Nicodemus were the more remarkable because spoken to him. He was no profligate sunk in the mire and filth of bestiality. Nor was he a self-centred and self-satisfied Pharisee. He was a sincere seeker after truth, and the question he put to Jesus revealed the working of his mind. He came to a Teacher from God, and therefore he came with an open mind willing to receive truth. He was perhaps the most perfect example of the highest possibilities of the old covenant, which had instructed men in the things of God and had led them to the highest act possible in the energy of fallen nature—that, namely, of submission to a baptism which symbolized repentance. Christ's answer cast no aspersion upon the past. It revealed its limitations. It was as though He had declared that John, the last of the magnificent line of the Hebrew prophets, had done all that was possible in leading unregenerate men to the door of the kingdom. To enter, there was necessary the new and essential miracle of Christianity—that man should have a second birth, without which he could neither see nor enter in. Times have not altered human nature, nor have they changed the essential character of Christianity. To every seeker Jesus still says: *Ye must be born anew.* The first chapter of the practical section of this book is therefore devoted to a study of the New Birth, its necessity, nature, evidence, and method.

The teaching of Christ was unified. He said in a sentence, what other teachers under the inspiration of the Holy Spirit, would unfold in volumes. This conversation with Nicodemus deals fully and finally with this whole subject. The teaching of the Epistles is, however, valuable, in order that the sayings of the Master may be fully comprehended.

As to the necessity for the new birth, He declared: *That which is born of the flesh is flesh.*[1] This statement must never be construed into a condemnation of the physical and material side of man's nature. That matter is inherently evil is a doctrine of devils, that finds no warrant in the teaching of Christ or His apostles. Every pulse and fibre of physical being owes its creation and preservation to the thought and power of God. That which He created in His own image, and which,

[1] John iii. 6.

when redeemed, He inhabits as a temple, is not in itself evil. The condition of human life apart from God is evil, because it has passed into limitation and prostitution. Those wondrous material bases of life upon which, for a time, essential being was to manifest itself, and be prepared for the final and perfected life, have become the prison-house of the spirit, and man is attempting to live by bread alone, to condition his being in the flesh. That is the condition of life which Jesus describes as flesh, and of that He says: *That which is born of the flesh is flesh.* The same guarding of terms is necessary in turning to the Epistles. The writers place the natural and spiritual in perpetual antithesis. This is not because the spiritual is unnatural, or the natural unspiritual. The deepest fact of human nature is that the natural is spiritual, and only when all the being is dominated by spirit is man natural. A concrete illustration may be found in the early chapters of Genesis. The man in the garden, himself a spirit tabernacling in physical dwelling, and yet holding unafraid communion with that God Who is a Spirit, is the natural man. He, who presently is seen bending back to earth, and entering upon the bread life which is ever through the sweat of the brow, is unnatural, because contrary to the Divine purpose and thought. When New Testament writers speak of the natural man, they are not condemning that which is natural in the sense now described. They are using the phrase in exactly the same way the Lord here used the word *flesh,* to describe the condition of being which is enslaved by the things temporal and material, as in opposition to those eternal and spiritual. This is the condition under which men are now born, and herein lies the necessity for the new birth.

What this condition really is may be gathered from a consideration of certain of the words of Paul. Take, first, his description of the Gentiles before they are brought into union with Christ: *Darkened in their understanding, alienated from the life of God.*[1] That is the root-trouble. Man has lost his vision of God. He has no true conception of God. Man has ever been attempting to construct a deity out of the imaginings of his own heart, and the result has been the idea of God as an enlarged man, and a consequent misconception of His true being. A flesh-conditioned life cannot discover God. Hence the necessity for the new birth, which is first of all new vision.

Then consider the apostle's description of the heart of the unregenerate: *The mind of the flesh is enmity against God.*[2] How man fears God—nay, hates Him! To disturb the peace and mar the pleasure of the worldling, it is only necessary to introduce a conversation concerning Divine things. The one constant and successful endeavour of the flesh-homed life is to keep God out of conscious touch. There may be no open blasphemy, no avowed hatred, but the unvarying law of life,

[1] Eph. iv. 18. [2] Rom. viii. 7.

and the unchanging order of its activities, reveal that man has no desire for God, no joy in His company. A flesh-conditioned life cannot love God. Hence the necessity for the new birth is that of a new possibility of love.

Again, notice the description the apostle gives of the purpose, and set, and impulse, of the unregenerate: *They that are after the flesh do mind the things of the flesh.*[1] It would be a startling revelation to some persons if they would take the time to examine their own lives for any given week, registering the occupation of all the hours. One hundred and sixty-eight hours in all, — so many given to the spiritual side of life, so many to the mental, so many to the purely physical; the vast majority devoted to *What shall we eat? . . . What shall we drink? . . . Wherewithal shall we be clothed?*[2] This is so in many and varied ways, and must continue until man is born of the Spirit, and a higher view of life, and consequently other impulses, are produced.

Once again, notice his statement concerning the true government of such lives: *Ye walked . . . according to the prince of the power of the air.*[3] They are the slaves of Satan, accomplishing his designs, yielding their allegiance to him. All unconsciously, man apart from God becomes the abject slave of the devil, and through the flesh hears the suggestions and proposals of hell. and yields to them, and becomes more and more fast bound.

[1] Rom. viii. 5. [2] Matt. vi. 31. [3] Eph. ii. 2.

This fourfold description explains the meaning of Jesus' words to Nicodemus, and gives the necessity for the new birth: *That which is born of the flesh is flesh.*[1] The understanding is darkened; the heart is at enmity; the life is set on the things of the flesh; the being is enslaved by Satan. The hopelessness of man is still more clearly seen when it is observed that this fourfold description is a sequence. The understanding dark, and therefore a false conception of God. Then it is not to be wondered at that man hates. No man could hate the true and living God. The hatred of the human heart is for the monster of its own imagination. There can be no love for God until all the false views are swept away by the new vision that breaks with the new birth. If man turn away from God in hatred, it follows that, in order to satisfy the craving of his nature, he will turn to fleshly things and earthly things, because he has no vision of the higher. The man with the muck-rake is proving his capacity for the unseen crown by the very devotion with which he is searching amid the baubles at his feet. There will be no deliverance until a new life gives him the sense of those higher possibilities. The man thus enslaved is enslaved by Satan. God's perpetual work is to bring man near to Himself, that man may love. Satan ever enslaves through agencies and intermediaries, lest man, seeing the corruption, should be afraid and escape. This is no flattering tale of the need

[1] John iii. 6.

of human nature, yet it is the account which alone is true to the facts of history, and the present state of men. There is neither light, nor life, nor love, nor liberty save in the power of the regeneration of the Holy Spirit. *Ye must be born anew,* for *that which is born of the flesh is flesh.*[1]

The nature of the change necessary is perhaps most sublimely described by the simplicity of the words of which Jesus made use: *Except a man be born anew.*[2] A birth is a beginning. It is not the reconstruction or renovation of something already in existence, but the commencement of a new thing. That is what a man needs, if he would see or enter the kingdom. This statement of the case immediately lifts the possibility of being a Christian out of the realm of the human as to initiation. God only can begin a new thing. Men may manipulate the things that are, may replace in another order, may imagine they have started, begun something; but give a man nothing and tell him to begin a new thing, and the only new thing will be the old nothing. Born: that is the supreme fact; it is the commencement. As every living being is a work of God, so, if there is to be new birth, that also must be of God. If man must be born anew, then is he helpless until the Spirit of God work the creative miracle.

This view of the Christian life as a new thing was that which the apostles clearly enforced: *If any man is in*

[1] John iii. 7, 6. [2] John iii. 3.

Christ, there is a new creation: the old things are passed away; behold, they are become new.[1] A new creation, having a new vision of God, out of which springs a new love for God and a new devotion to Him—this is beyond the possibility of analysis. It is the mystery of life, and, like every other phase and form of life, is beyond the explanation of any teacher or scientist the world has produced.

The result of the new birth Christ declares as clearly and as simply in the second half of the verse first quoted: *That which is born of the Spirit is spirit.*[2] Again it must be restated that He is not undervaluing the physical side of man's being, and certainly He is not putting it out of count altogether. The vision presented by the statement is that of human life in which first things are first, and second things are second, and last things are last—life in which spirit is dominant, the lord of being, and soul and body are subservient and sanctified. It is a perfect contrast to the old life; but it is a contrast which consists, not in the exaltation of one side of the being at the expense of the others, but in the restoration of the true balance of power and proportion. The change is summarized in the words of Christ, and light is thrown again upon this summary from the Epistles.

Following a law of nature, Christ placed the antidote in juxtaposition to the poison. Immediately after His summary of the facts of human life in the words *That*

[1] 2 Cor. v. 17 (margin). [2] John iii. 6.

which is born of the flesh, is flesh, He gave as brief and graphic a description of the changed life: *That which is born of the Spirit is spirit.* This method is followed through the New Testament, and a second reference to the statements of the apostle concerning the natural man will reveal a statement in each case side by side with them, giving the antitheses in the spiritual man. Those *darkened in their understanding* become *taught in Him, even as truth is in Jesus.*[1] Those of whom it was declared that *the mind of the flesh is enmity against God,*[2] being born again of the Spirit, and indwelt by the Spirit, look into the face of God and cry, *Abba, Father.* They that being *after the flesh* did *mind the things of the flesh,* now being *after the Spirit* do mind *the things of the Spirit.*[3] Those who *walked . . . according to the prince of the power of the air,*[4] now *sit with Him in the heavenly places, in Christ Jesus.*[5]

The whole form and fashion of the life is changed, and the change is so radical and complete that the only way in which it is possible to account for it, is by the acceptation of the teaching of Christ, that it has been brought about by a new creation, a new beginning, a new birth.

As there was a sequence of thought in the description of man's condition in his sinful nature, so also is there in the antitheses just glanced at. The first effect of im-

[1] Eph. iv. 18, 21. [2] Rom. viii. 7. [3] Rom. viii. 15, 5. [4] Eph. ii. 2. [5] Eph. ii. 6.

parted life is to give man a true vision of God. That which could not be found by the flesh life is discovered directly the new life restores the lost sight. Then the spirit of man, seeing God, cries, *Father.* Fear passes, and the life—tremblingly, it may be, at the beginning, but none the less surely—takes hold upon God with intense satisfaction and ever-deepening love. That is the cure for the minding of earthly things. To revert to a former illustration, let but the man with the muck-rake see the higher things and know they are his own, he will forget all the empty trifles that have captivated him before. Again, the man satisfied with the things of God, becomes, by that very sense of satisfaction, master of Satan, and invulnerable against all his attacks.

The method of the new birth is most definitely stated in this same conversation. The miracle itself is a Divine work. The condition upon which it is wrought is the point of human responsibility. In the words *born of the Spirit* the Master claims the essential act as Divine, and most clearly does He show that work to be beyond our comprehension. *The wind bloweth where it listeth, and thou hearest the voice thereof, but knowest not whence it cometh, and whither it goeth: so is every one that is born of the Spirit.*[1] Just as the power of the wind is beyond dispute by the evidences of its blowing that appeal to the senses, while the law of its coming and going abides a mystery, so the fact of the regenerating

[1] John iii. 8.

power of the Holy Spirit is proved by the phenomena of grace, while all the sacred mystery of its operation is beyond the discovery of any human mind. Men are called upon to accept the fact in each case, and to wait for the explanation of the mystery. Granted the possibility of the miracle, it is for man to seek to know the condition upon which it is wrought. This Nicodemus felt, and hence his question: *How can these things be?*[1] The answer is perfectly clear: *And as Moses lifted up the serpent in the wilderness, even so must the Son of Man be lifted up: that whosoever believeth may in Him have eternal life.*[2] Man needs life. The Son of Man is to be lifted up that it may be provided. Pointing this seeker to the kingdom, the Master sets His Cross as the gate of life. On the place of awful uplifting, through the mystery of His Passion, He would liberate His life that this man might share it. The life-giving work of the Spirit is to be that of communicating to souls, dead in trespasses and sins, the very life of the Son of God. This can only be done as the corn of wheat dies to live, and there is no new birth for individuals or the race, but by the death of the Son of Man. That death has been accomplished, and now *whosoever believeth may in Him have eternal life.* The one condition of life is that of belief. What this belief is has explanation in the opening part of this Gospel: *But as many as received Him, to them gave He the right to become children of*

[1] John iii. 9. [2] John iii. 14, 15.

God, even to them that believe on His name.[1] Here two terms are used in explanation of each other. To believe on Him is to receive Him: to receive Him is to believe on His name. To believe is the condition upon which the Holy Spirit imparts the life by the coming of which old things pass away, all things are new. Thousands believe in the historic Christ, and are yet dead in trespasses and sins. No weak trembling soul in all the centuries has ever yet believed on Him in the sense of receiving Him as the Way, the Truth, the Life, with unquestioning surrender and abandonment, but immediately the new life has been imparted. In this, as in everything, God is a God of method, and this is His law of grace, by observance of which man appropriates the blessings of the Cross.

Ye must be born anew.[2] Apart from this there is no escape *from the corruption that is in the world by lust.*[3] Save through this, there is no becoming *partakers of the Divine nature.* While living in the full tide of spiritual possibilities, men shall yet pass through the years of probation barren and dead, unless they surrender to the Infinite Love; and receiving Him Whom they crucified in blindness, become *heirs of God, and joint-heirs with Christ.*[4]

[1] John i. 12. [2] John iii. 7. [3] 2 Pet. i. 4. [4] Rom. viii. 17.

XIX

BE FILLED WITH THE SPIRIT

THEY fall far short of the truth who speak of the filling of the Spirit as the privilege of believers. The word of Paul *Be not drunken with wine, wherein is riot, but be filled with the Spirit,*[1] is a present imperative, being of the nature of a command, rather than a counsel of perfection. Not merely for an elect few, but for all those born of the Spirit, the will of God is that they should be filled with the Spirit. And the necessity for this filling is proved by the fact that, apart from it, there can be no full Christian life, and no powerful Christian service.

The apostle declares that *no man speaking in the Spirit of God saith, Jesus is anathema; and no man can say, Jesus is Lord, but in the Holy Spirit.*[2] The Lordship of Jesus is the basis of all Christian life. The Christian graces and virtues all spring from the recognition of that Lordship, and from absolute surrender thereto. It is only as man is born again of the Spirit that he can call Jesus Lord; and it is only as he is under

[1] Eph. v. 18. [2] 1 Cor. xii. 3.

the perfect dominion of that Spirit that he can live under the Lordship of Jesus.

Not only is this true with regard to the first step in life, but also in reference to the whole subsequent course. *The fruit of the Spirit is love, joy, peace, longsuffering, kindness, goodness, faithfulness, meekness, temperance: against such there is no law.*[1] These are the evidences of Christian character looked for in all those who profess to belong to Christ, the things that differentiate between a Christly and a worldly soul. There can be no manifestation of them save under the perpetual control of the Spirit. Neither is it possible to work for God except in the energy of the Spirit. There may be a great deal of what appears to be Christian work, but it is absolutely devoid of power unless thus energized.

No man can live the Christian life, and no man can serve in the Christian dispensation, save as he is filled with the Spirit.

It is, then, of urgent importance that there should be clear understanding of the law which governs this filling. That there are scores of Christian people who are not filled with the Holy Spirit is an all too evident fact. Bring that cluster of the wonderful *fruit of the Spirit* side by side with the actual life and achievement of scores of professing Christians, and this fact must be at once confessed.

[1] Gal. v. 22, 23.

To Christian people who really want to be such as God would have them be, who are tired of all that is merely formal and mediocre, and are anxious to live in the will of God at all costs, there is no question of more importance than that of the conditions upon which the believer, born of the Spirit, may live that life which is filled with the Spirit.

These conditions are of a twofold nature,—the initial, and the continuous; that by which blessing is first realized, and that by which it is maintained.

The first is that of abandonment.

The second is that of abiding.

The word *abandonment* is used intentionally. Consecration is a great word, but it has been so much abused that it has lost much of its deepest significance. This word *abandonment* is perhaps out of the ordinary run of theological terms, but it is full of force. Wherever whole-hearted, absolute, unquestioning, positive, final abandonment of the life to God obtains, the life becomes filled with the Spirit.

The thought is contained in Paul's words: *Neither present your members unto sin as instruments of unrighteousness; but present yourselves unto God, as alive from the dead, and your members as instruments of righteousness unto God.*[1] The whole life, according to this conception, is to be handed over to the control of God, in order that, through that life, His will may be

[1] Rom. vi. 13.

realized, His work may be done, His plans may be carried out. That is the abandoned life.

There are two passages which bear on this subject. The first reads: *Grieve not the Holy Spirit of God, in Whom ye were sealed unto the day of redemption. Let all bitterness, and wrath, and anger, and clamor, and railing, be put away from you, with all malice.*[1] This is the abandonment of the life for purification. Abandonment to God is not merely the act of enlisting as soldiers to fight battles—that is a secondary matter; it is first the abandonment of self to the Spirit of God, that He may purify and cleanse from everything that is unlike His own perfection of beauty.

The apostle did not say: *Put away bitterness, and wrath, and anger, and clamour, and railing.* The believer is not called upon to put these things out of the life: that is not the New Testament conception of purification. He said: *Let these things be put away.* The verse preceding explains the responsibility: *Grieve not the Holy Spirit.* The work of putting out of the life this unholy brood of evil things—bitterness, wrath, anger, clamour, railing—is not man's work. Man is to let Him accomplish it.

The second passage is as familiar as the first: *I beseech you therefore, brethren, by the mercies of God, to present your bodies a living sacrifice, holy, acceptable to God, which is your reasonable service.*[2] This is an-

[1] Eph. iv. 30, 31. [2] Rom. xii. 1.

other aspect of abandonment. It is not merely assent to purification; it is also the presentation of the whole being to God for sacrifice. There are very many who seem to imagine that the apostle is calling Christians to sacrifice themselves to God, but he is rather calling upon them to present themselves to God as a sacrifice, which the High Priest will lay upon the altar. The abandonment asked for is a twofold one,—first, abandonment to purification by the Spirit; and, secondly, abandonment of the whole being to Jesus Christ, that He may offer it to God.

The theory seems easy. The practice is a very definite thing. The life which is thus abandoned to God for the filling of the Spirit is a life that has given up its own plans, and purposes, and hopes; and has taken instead the plan, and the purpose, and the hope of God.

If God wills to alter what appear to be Divine arrangements for to-day, so that the desire and the hope of to-day are disappointed, the follower of the Master should yet be able to say: *I delight to do Thy will, O my God.*[1] The will of God should be the supreme matter, beyond the doing of which the soul should have no anxiety. How often men promise God that they will do certain things if He will do something for them! —an iniquitous attempt to bargain with the Most High, which is very popular, and as old as Jacob.

The difference between the Spirit-filled life, and the

[1] Ps. xl. 8.

life that is not filled with the Spirit, is the difference between a life abandoned wholly to the will of God, and a life that wants to have its own way and please God too. Abandonment is that of which it is most easy to speak, and yet it is the one thing from which all men shrink. Men are quite prepared to sign pledges, to do any amount of work, even to sign cheques or give money, if only God will let them have their own way somewhere in their life. If He will not press this business of abandonment, if He will not bring them to the Cross, they will do anything; but they draw back from the place of death.

Yet it is only in that place that the Holy Spirit is able to flow out into every part of the life and energize it, until in all conduct Jesus is crowned Lord, and the fruit of the Spirit is manifest in character. Nothing can take the place of abandonment. Some there are who attempt to put prayer where God has put abandonment. Others profess to be waiting until God is willing to fill them. Both are wrong! While they think they are waiting for God, the fact is God is waiting for them. At any moment, if they yield to the Spirit, He will sweep through every gate and avenue and into every corner of the life.

The filling of the Spirit is retained by abiding in Christ. A great deal has been said about abiding, and many have endeavoured to define the term. Some beautiful definitions have been given, mystical and poetical, and yet for the most part out of the reach of the ordinary life of the believer.

It is well, where possible, to have definitions of Scripture from Scripture; and John gives a definition of what it is to abide in Christ: *He that keepeth His commandments abideth in Him, and He in him.*[1] Nothing can be simpler. The mistake which may be made is that of trying to explain that passage until it is robbed of its simplicity. The definition is the very embodiment of clearness, and may be stated in a brief sentence: To abide is to obey.

The *commandments* referred to are given in the preceding passage; but are spoken of there, as one commandment, having two applications: *And this is His commandment, that we should believe in the name of His Son Jesus Christ, and love one another.*[2] The whole law of Jesus Christ is summed up in that verse. The commandment is that of faith and love. Faith is the absolute dependence of the soul upon Him, and the consequent life of obedience to Him. Faith in the Lord Jesus begins when a guilty soul submits itself to Him for pardon; but it does not end then. It is not by that one act of faith that men abide, but by continuing in the course begun, by making Him Lord always,—by entering into no transaction of business or of pleasure without taking Him into account; by treating Him as the ever-present King, by believing in Him; and by

[1] 1 John iii. 24. [2] 1 John iii. 23.

saying to Him, at all seasons and hours and everywhere: *Master, is this Thy will?* Faith in Him is belief on His name at the beginning for pardon, and constantly for purity and direction. Then every moment the soul lives in dependence upon Christ, and is able to sing:

I dare not take one step without Thy aid.

Not faith merely, but love: *That we should . . . love one another.*[1] That is the life of service. *He that keepeth His commandments abideth in Him.* The conditions for abiding in Him are those of always believing in Him, always loving some one and serving some one. If men are filled with the Spirit by abandonment, they continue filled with the Spirit by abiding.

While it is true that there can be no full life and no powerful service apart from the filling of the Spirit, it is equally true that the Spirit-filled life must manifest the fruit of the Spirit and be powerful in service for God. These broad principles, however, are granted. The present subject is rather the conscious experience of a soul that is filled with the Spirit. Here a word of warning is necessary. A vital mistake is made by persons who formulate a code of sensations, and wait for them as evidences of the Spirit's filling. Some expect a magnetic thrill, some an overwhelming ecstasy. These experiences may be realized, they may be utterly absent. Others wait for an experience like that of some

[1] 1 John iii. 23, 24.

one else. That they will never have. There are many people who have read the Lives of good men like Fletcher of Madeley, Finney, and Bowen, and who expect to realize just what these men describe. Such hopes are doomed to disappointment. It may safely be said that the experience of the filling of the Spirit is in no two cases exactly identical, any more than the consciousness of ordinary life can ever be the same in any two persons. There are points of resemblance, great fundamental facts which are identical; but in the light and shade there is variety. Surely, if this be true of ordinary life, it is also true of the higher spiritual blessing. The Holy Spirit fills one and another. The realization of the one differs from that of the other. *There are diversities of workings, but the same God.*[1]

There is, however, a common consciousness to those who are Spirit-filled. It is the consciousness of Christ. The Holy Spirit, coming in His fulness, will give men to know the Lord as they never knew Him before. The consciousness of Christ in the experience of believers will be as varied as are the saints themselves; for the full consciousness of the Head can only be realized by the whole Church. His greatness is such that He cannot give Himself wholly and utterly and finally to an individual; He needs the whole Church for the display of His perfect glory, and the unfolding of the majesty of His Person. Let no one narrow down his

[1] 1 Cor. xii. 6.

consciousness of the Christ to the consciousness of any single person. He is one thing to one man, He is another thing to another, but the men are united in the fact that it is the Master of Whom they are all conscious by the Spirit. The Lordship of Jesus as a reality, is the first result of the Spirit-filled life.

It follows that Christ's victory over evil will be shared by His people; His point of vision of the affairs of men and the needs of men will be theirs also; and the impulses of service which bore Him to Calvary, against all opposition, and made Him Victor in its darkest hour, will likewise be their impulse of service, so that no longer will they offer Him the service of mechanical arrangement; but in the passion of His life they will serve, even though that be a consuming passion, as it was with Him.

Again, Christ's revelation of God to men will in measure be their revelation of God to men. As the Spirit fills the children of God, He will reproduce in their lives such likeness to Christ, that men, seeing them, will begin to understand Him, and be led into a clear apprehension of the glory of the Father.

This subject brings all to the point of personal responsibility. The whole study culminates here for the individual. That Divine Spirit Who worked in creation, who was the Spirit of revelation and of service through every age, dwells now in each believer. The individual question is whether He is indwelling in all

His fulness. Or is He grieved and quenched by disloyalty to His government? If that has been the case hitherto, let the whole life be yielded to Him, that He may reproduce the Master Himself, to the glory of God, and for the good of men.

XX

RESIST NOT, GRIEVE NOT, QUENCH NOT

NEW privileges always bring new responsibilities; and it follows, necessarily and naturally, that these new responsibilities create new perils. If this age is the most favoured in the history of men, it has therefore to face greatest and gravest perils. They are the perils of resisting, grieving, and quenching the Spirit. The terms do not refer to the same danger. There are those who have not resisted the Spirit who yet are grieving Him; there are also those who have not resisted and have not grieved Him in the sense in which the apostles used the word, who are nevertheless in perpetual danger of quenching Him. The peril of resisting the Spirit is that of those who are not born again; the peril of grieving the Spirit is that of those who, born of the Spirit, are indwelt by Him; the peril of quenching the Spirit is that of those upon whom He has bestowed some gift for service.

To Nicodemus Jesus said: *Ye must be born anew.*[1]

[1] John iii. 7.

That refers to the first act of the Spirit in man. To the woman of Samaria He said: *Whosoever drinketh of the water that I shall give him shall never thirst; but the water that I shall give him shall become in him a well of water springing up unto eternal life.*[1] That refers to the second aspect of the Spirit's work in the believer, as a perennial and perpetual spring. To the crowds at the feast He said: *He that believeth on Me, as the scripture hath said, out of his belly shall flow rivers of living water.*[2] That refers to the work of the Spirit, in its outflow through the believer, for the refreshment and renewal of other lives.

The three aspects of the Spirit's work, regeneration, indwelling, and equipment, reveal the perils of the dispensation.

In reference to regeneration the peril is marked by the word *resist.* In reference to indwelling the peril is marked by the word *grieve.* In reference to equipment for service the peril is marked by the word *quench.*

The first of these words occurs in the defence of Stephen. After having enumerated the acts of rebellion which had characterized the history of his people, he exclaimed: *Ye stiffnecked and uncircumcised in heart and ears, ye do always resist the Holy Spirit.*[3] Resisting the Holy Spirit consisted in a determined hostility to His purposes and work. At the moment it was not always apparently wilful; the sin lay in the fact that

[1] John iv. 14. [2] John vii. 38. [3] Acts vii. 51.

they did not perceive their opportunity when it came. When his brethren sold Joseph, they did not understand that they were selling their deliverer into slavery. It was a sin of blindness. When the people failed to understand Moses, and refused him, and murmured against him, they did not comprehend all the Divine mission for which he was raised. They were hostile to the work of the Holy Spirit of God, and their hostility was the result of blindness. Resisting the Holy Spirit, therefore, is not necessarily wilful—it may be the result of blindness; but when God deals with men, He takes into account that which causes the blindness, and where the cause is of their own creation, He holds them responsible. Jealousy and hatred blinded the brethren of Joseph to his true position; and the same spirit of malice lay at the root of the opposition to Moses. They were blinded, and out of the blindness grew the hostility. The reason for the blindness was disobedience to the heavenly vision at some earlier point in their history; and for that disobedience they were guilty.

Men need perpetually to examine themselves as to whether they are in the faith. There are many who would vehemently deny the charge of being hostile to Divine purposes, whose lives are out of all harmony with the movements of the Spirit. He Who has come to set up in the heart of man the kingdom of God, He Who has come to bring righteousness and love into human lives as forces that transform and transfigure, has not yet been able to accomplish these purposes in them. By so much as that is a fact the Holy Spirit is being resisted. To the Corinthians the apostle wrote: *Try your own selves, whether ye be in the faith.*[1] It is a solemn warning, occurring as it does after the expression of a fear on his part: *I fear, lest by any means, when I come, I should find you not such as I would, and should myself be found of you such as ye would not; lest by any means there should be strife, jealousy, wraths, factions, backbitings, whisperings, swellings, tumults.*[2] The whole unholy brood may be summed up in the one thought of lack of love. Among the things of which the apostle was afraid, there were none which were deeds of open impurity. It was the spirit of faction, schism, and division that he feared; and his fear gave rise to his warning. *Try your own selves, whether ye be in the faith.* That was a word spoken, not to the outside world, but to professing Christians. The question as to whether men are resisting the Spirit, as to whether they are a part of the force that is hostile to the Spirit in the world, is to be settled, not by the judgment that neighbours pass, but by the judgment that falls clear as the light and searching as fire, when in the place of loneliness with God the prayer is sincerely offered:

Search me, O God, and know my heart:
Try me, and know my thoughts:
And see if there be any way of wickedness in me.[3]

[1] 2 Cor. xiii. 5. [2] 2 Cor. xii. 20. [3] Ps. cxxxix. 23, 24.

There is perpetual need for rigorous self-examination as to whether those professing loyalty are still in the faith; for it may be that, by disloyalty to God, the mind has been blinded to the correct perception of the work of the Spirit; and without intending it, there may be hostility to His work, there may even be resistance to the Holy Spirit.

The second peril is that of *grieving* the Holy Spirit. There is no word in the New Testament that more clearly and beautifully reveals the tenderness of the heart of God. The word means literally, *to cause sorrow to.* Dr. Beet has said that the word *grieve* is one of the most striking instances of anthropomorphism in the whole Book. It certainly is a remarkable instance of the way in which God graciously uses the being of man for the illustration of His own activity of affection and thought. There is a sense in which it is difficult to think of God as sorrowing; and yet He stoops to this great word, to teach that it is possible for a child of His, indwelt by the Spirit, to cause sorrow to His heart. Let no one minimize the value of the word. Grieve not, do not cause sorrow to, do not make sad the heart of God.

The words occur in the midst of a most magnificent argument concerning the high calling of God for His people, and are connected with the statement: *In Whom ye also, having heard the word of the truth, the gospel of your salvation,—in Whom, having also believed, ye were sealed with the Holy Spirit of promise, which is an earnest of our inheritance, unto the redemption of God's own possesssion, unto the praise of His glory.*[1] The Holy Spirit seals the believer unto the day of redemption. When He takes up His abode in the heart of the trusting soul, it is not only for present blessing, it is also for a consummation. When the Holy Spirit takes possession of a soul and imparts life, that life is the prophecy and the promise of an eventuality. For those who are children of God, the full meaning of the fact is not yet: *Beloved, now are we children of God, and it is not yet made manifest what we shall be. We know that, if He shall be manifested, we shall be like Him.*[2] What the glory of the coming One will be, none can imagine; nor can they yet know what will be the glory of the children of God, when the work of God is finished in their lives. The Holy Spirit within, seals unto that glorious issue. The sealing consists not merely in setting a possession mark upon the property, but in the outworking in the life of all the beauty and all the grace of Christ Himself. As when our blessed Lord was transfigured upon the mountain it was not the transfiguring of a glory that fell upon Him, but that of a glory that was already resident within Him, outshining through the veil of His flesh,—so, when the Spirit seals, He does so by the gift of life, which is able to transform the character.

Out of that second aspect of the work of the Spirit grows the second peril. Whenever He is thwarted,

[1] Eph. i, 13, 14. [2] 1 John iii. 2.

whenever He is disobeyed, whenever He gives some new revelation of the Christ which brings no response, He is grieved. The heart of God is sad when, by the disobedience of His children, His purpose of grace in them is hindered. Alas! how often has the Holy Spirit been grieved; how often has He brought some vision of the Master that has made demands upon devotion, that has claimed new consecration; and because the way of devotion and the way of consecration are always the way of the Altar and the Cross, the children of His love have drawn back. The Spirit has been grieved, because hindered in His purposes; the day of the saints' perfecting has been postponed, and the coming of the kingdom of God has been delayed. It is a very terrible thought that the grieving of the Spirit within the Church postpones the coming of the kingdom of God in the world. In proportion as men are obedient to the indwelling Spirit, and allow Him in the whole territory of their own lives to have His way, in that proportion are they hastening the coming of the day of God, and bringing in the Kingdom of Peace.

The things which grieve the Spirit of God are spoken of by the apostle in the section of the Epistle from which this warning is taken, and should be pondered in solemn loneliness.

The third and last peril is that described in the words: *Quench not the Spirit.*[1] The word *quench* has no reference to the indwelling of the Spirit for life and de-

[1] 1 Thess. v. 19.

velopment in the believer. It refers wholly to His presence as a power in service. The word itself is suggestive. To resist presupposes the coming of the Holy Spirit to storm the citadel of the soul. To grieve presupposes the residence of the Spirit as the Comforter within. The word *quench* presupposes the presence of the Spirit as a fire. This suggestion of fire carries thought back to the words: *There appeared unto them tongues parting asunder, like as of fire; and it sat upon each one of them.*[1] Fire was the symbol of power to praise, to pray, and to prophesy. Moreover, the context of this injunction clearly indicates its meaning. In the argument of the apostle two things are linked: *Quench not the Spirit; despise not prophesyings.*[2] Here, then, is the third peril. The Spirit, Who comes upon the believer for praise, prayer, and prophecy, may be quenched. It is possible that the gift of the Holy Spirit, bestowed for service, may be lost; it is possible that those upon whom there has fallen, unseen by mortal eye, the Tongue of Fire, who have been called by God to the place of actual service in the Church, may quench the Spirit, and thus lose their power of testimony.

This is done by reversing the conditions upon which the Spirit was received. The apostles first received the Spirit of Fire upon the condition of loyalty to Jesus Christ. The glorifying of Christ in the life, and the obedience of the soul to the word of the Master, were

[1] Acts ii. 3. [2] 1 Thess. v. 19, 20.

the first conditions for the falling of the Fire. That included within itself the second condition of human helplessness, confessed by their waiting until the Holy Spirit came.

There has been much quenching of the Holy Spirit by service that does not wait but rushes, and by the burning of false fires upon the altars of God. The attempt to carry on the work of the kingdom of God by worldly means, the perpetual desecration of holy things by alliance with things that are unholy, the pressing of Mammon into the service of God, have meant the quenching of the Spirit; for God will never allow the Fire of the Holy Spirit to be mingled with strange fires upon His altars. What is true of the Churches is true of the individual. God has equipped His people for service with spiritual gifts. To each one some Fire-gift of speech or of influence has been given; but it has been lost, when it has ceased to be used in loyalty to Christ. Very many men have lost their gift of power in service, and have become barren of results in their work for God, because they have prostituted a heavenly gift to sordid, selfish service, to the glorification of their own lives, instead of exercising the gift only for its true end. Men have perpetually quenched the Spirit by attempting to work in their own strength, hoping that God would step in and make up what they lacked. God will not come and help men to do their work. He asks that they should give themselves to Him, for the doing of His work. This is no mere idle play upon words; the difference is radical. If men make their plan of service and then ask God to help them, they may, by that very assertion of self, quench the Holy Spirit. If, on the other hand, they await the Divine vision and the Divine voice and the Divinely marked out path; if they wait until they hear God saying, *I am going there, I would have you go with Me,*—then the Holy Spirit can exercise His gift in their lives. The Spirit is quenched by disloyalty to Christ, or when His gift is used for any other purposes than that upon which the heart of God is set. *Resist not, grieve not, quench not the Spirit!*

The deep meaning of these solemn warnings may the Spirit Himself reveal to all the Spirit-born children of the Father.